Editor
Eric Migliaccio

Managing Editor
Ina Massler Levin, M.A.

Editor-in-Chief
Sharon Coan, M.S. Ed.

Cover Art
Barb Lorseyedi

Illustrator
Kevin McCarthy

Art Manager
Kevin Barnes

Art Director
CJae Froshay

Imaging
James Edward Grace
Rosa C. See

Product Manager
Phil Garcia

Ideas contributed by
Jeanne Dustman, M. Ed.

Publisher
Mary D. Smith, M.S. Ed.

Reading First
Activities

Grade 2

- Phonemic Awareness
- Phonics
- Fluency
- Vocabulary
- Comprehension

Author

Jennifer Overend Prior, Ph.D.

Teacher Created Resources

Teacher Created Resources, Inc.
6421 Industry Way
Westminster, CA 92683
www.teachercreated.com
ISBN-0-7439-3022-3
©2004 Teacher Created Resources, Inc.
Reprinted, 2005
Made in U.S.A.

Table of Contents

Introduction

More than ever before, children's development of reading skills has come to the forefront of education in the United States. The National Reading Panel (2000) presented a report entitled, "Teaching Children to Read: An Evidence-Based Assessment of the Scientific Research Literature on Reading and Its Implications for Reading Instruction—Reports of Subgroups." This report reflects reading research—focusing on kindergarten through grade three—and targets methods of instruction that lead to reading success. The panel's report highlights the following elements of reading:

- ✧ **Phonemic Awareness**
- ✧ **Phonics**
- ✧ **Fluency**
- ✧ **Vocabulary**
- ✧ **Comprehension**

This book serves to provide teachers with practical strategies for teaching reading skills in these areas.

The terminology below is commonly used when discussing reading instruction and will be helpful in understanding and discussing the five elements of reading.

✧ Phonemic Awareness

- **phonemic awareness**—an individual's ability to attend to the sounds of spoken words
- **phonological awareness**—ability to recognize phonemes, graphemes, rhymes, syllables, etc.
- **phonemes**—sounds in spoken language
- **graphemes**—the smallest part of written language
- **phonics**—relationship between the sounds and symbols of spoken and written language
- **syllable**—part of a word that contains a vowel or vowel sound
- **onset**—the initial consonant in a syllable
- **rime**—the syllable part that contains a vowel
      (Example: In *dog*, the onset is *d*, and the rime is *og*.)

✧ Phonics

- **synthetic phonics**—the ability to convert letters into sounds and blend them together
- **analytic phonics**—the ability to analyze the letters and sounds in words
- **analogy-based phonics**—using knowledge of word families to read unfamiliar words
- **phonics through spelling**—the ability to break words into sounds for writing
- **embedded phonics**—the instruction of letters and sounds within text
- **onset-rime phonics**—instruction that involves the identification of the initial sound in a word part (onset) and the remaining part of the word (rime)

Introduction *(cont.)*

◇ **Fluency**

- **fluency**—reading quickly and accurately
- **automaticity**—the quick recognition of words

◇ **Vocabulary**

- **specific word instruction**—the teaching of individual words
- **word-learning strategies**—the instruction of strategies that help children determine word meaning
- **word parts**—using parts of words (prefixes, suffixes, base words) to determine meanings of words
- **context clues**—surrounding phrases, sentences, and words that provide hints that lead to a word's meaning

◇ **Comprehension**

- **metacognition**—thinking about one's thinking or the ability to identify what is known and not known when reading
- **semantic organizers**—maps or webs used to illustrate the connection between concepts or ideas
- **direct explanation**—a teacher's explanation of the use of comprehension strategies
- **modeling**—teacher demonstration of the use of strategies
- **guided practice**—guidance by the teacher as a student applies strategies
- **application**—student practice of reading strategies

◇ **General Terminology**

- **explicit instruction**—direct instruction of strategies by the teacher
- **implicit instruction**—indirect instruction, often embedded in context

This book is divided into five sections featuring each of the elements of reading. Within each section you'll find activities for teacher-directed instruction, as well as small group and individual practice of reading skills. Many of the activities include follow-up games and reproducibles intended to provide additional practice of skills. The use of these activities, games, and practice sheets in addition to your comprehensive reading program will give your students the necessary skills for reading success.

Meeting Reading Standards

The chart below and on page 6 displays the McREL standards for reading in grades K–2. Used with permission from McREL (copyright 2000 McREL, Mid-continent Research for Education and Learning. 2550 S. Parker Road, Suite 500, Aurora, CO 80014. Telephone: 303-337-0990. Web site: *www.mcrel.org/standards-benchmarks).* The checks indicate the standards that are addressed by activities in this book. You will see a standards/objectives citation below each activity in this book.

Standard 5: Uses the general skills and strategies of the reading process	
1. Understands that print conveys meaning (i.e., knows that printed letters and words represent spoken language)	✓
2. Understands how print is organized and read (e.g., identifies front and back covers, title page, author, and illustrator; follows words from left to right and from top to bottom; knows the significance of spaces between words, knows the difference between letters, words, and sentences; understands the use of capitalization and punctuation as text boundaries)	
3. Creates mental images from pictures and print	
4. Uses meaning clues (e.g., pictures, picture captions, title, cover, headings, story structure, story topic) to aid comprehension and make predictions about content (e.g., action, events, character's behavior)	✓
5. Uses basic elements of phonetic analysis (e.g., common letter/sound relationships, beginning and ending consonants, vowel sounds, blends, word patterns) to decode unknown words	✓
6. Uses basic elements of structural analysis (e.g., syllables, basic prefixes, suffixes, root words, compound words, spelling patterns, contractions) to decode unknown words	✓
7. Uses a picture dictionary to determine word meaning	
8. Understands level-appropriate sight words and vocabulary (e.g., words for persons, places, things, actions; high-frequency words, such as *said*, *was*, and *where*)	✓
9. Uses self-correction strategies (e.g., searches for cues, identifies miscues, rereads, asks for help)	✓
10. Reads aloud familiar stories, poems, and passages with fluency and expression (e.g., rhythm, flow, meter, tempo, pitch, tone, intonation)	✓

Meeting Reading Standards *(cont.)*

The chart below is a continuation of the chart on page 5 that displays the McREL standards for reading in grades K–2. The checks indicate the standards that are addressed by activities in this book. You will see a standards/objectives citation below each activity in this book.

Standard 6: Uses reading skills and strategies to understand and interpret a variety of literary texts	
1. Uses reading skills and strategies to understand a variety of familiar literary passages and texts (e.g., fairy tales, folktales, fiction, nonfiction, legends, fables, myths, poems, nursery rhymes, picture books, predictable books)	✔
2. Knows setting, main characters, main events, sequence, and problems in stories	✔
3. Makes simple inferences regarding the order of events and possible outcomes	✔
4. Knows the main ideas or theme of a story	✔
5. Relates stories to personal experiences (e.g., events, characters, conflicts, themes)	✔

Standard 7: Uses reading skills and strategies to understand and interpret a variety of informational texts	
1. Uses reading skills and strategies to understand a variety of informational texts (e.g., written directions, signs, captions, warning labels, informational books)	
2. Understands the main idea and supporting details of simple expository information	✔
3. Summarizes information found in texts (e.g., retells in own words)	✔
4. Relates new information to prior knowledge and experience	✔

Phonemic Awareness

The term *phonemic awareness* refers to an individual's ability to attend to the sounds of spoken words. In order to begin to read, a child needs to understand that words are made up of individual sounds. It is important to remember that phonemic awareness activities should be fun and playful for the children.

Why Teach Phonemic Awareness?

Research suggests that experience with and instruction of phonemic awareness benefits children in their quest to become readers. Phonemic awareness assists children in spelling and should be related to letters in order to assist them with transitioning from hearing sounds to reading words.

You will notice that this section of the book is somewhat shorter than the others, as most children in grade 2 have already developed phonemic awareness. It is likely, however, that some of your students will still need practice in this area, which is why these activities have been included. You may want to incorporate these playful activities as a part of a whole-class routine.

As described in the report of The National Reading Panel, there are several elements involved in phonemic-awareness instruction. These include phoneme isolation, phoneme identity, phoneme categorization, phoneme blending, phoneme segmentation, phoneme deletion, phoneme addition, and phoneme substitution.

- ➤ **Phoneme Isolation** (recognizing sounds in words)
  - Example: The first sound in *dog* is /d/.

- ➤ **Phoneme Identity** (recognizing words that have similar sounds)
  - Example: The words *cat*, *car*, and *cave* all begin with /c/.

- ➤ **Phoneme Categorization** (recognizing words that sound the same and words that sound different)
  - Example: The words *bun*, *run*, and *fun* have similar sounds. The word *bat* does not sound the same.

- ➤ **Phoneme Blending** (combining spoken phonemes into words)
  - Example: The sounds /t/ /u/ /g/ make the word *tug*.

- ➤ **Phoneme Segmentation** (breaking words into their separate phonemes)
  - Example: There are four sounds in the word *truck*: /t/ /r/ /u/ /k/.

- ➤ **Phoneme Deletion** (identifying a new word when a phoneme is removed from another word)
  - Example: If you take away the /s/ in *start*, you have the word *tart*.

- ➤ **Phoneme Addition** (identifying a new word when a phoneme is added to another word)
  - Example: If you add /s/ to the beginning of *port*, you have the word *sport*.

- ➤ **Phoneme Substitution** (changing a phoneme in a word to make a new word)
  - Example: If you change the /r/ in *car* to /t/, you have the word *cat*.

When facilitating phonemic-awareness activities, focus only on one or two of these elements at a time. Keep in mind, also, that you may teach phonemic awareness in a variety of formats—whole-group, small-group, or individual instruction. You will need to determine which format best suits the needs of your students.

Phoneme-Isolation Activities

Phoneme isolation is the ability to recognize the sounds in words.

Names, Names, Names
Standard: 5.1

1. Gather your students together for a name game.

2. Ask each child to tell the sound that is heard at the beginning of his or her name. For example, the name *Jennifer* begins with the sound /j/.

3. After students identify the sounds at the beginning of their names, instruct them to organize themselves into groups based on the sounds at the beginning of their names. For example, all of the students with /m/ at the beginning stand together.

4. Be sure to discuss the fact that some letters make the same sound. For example, the names *Kylie* and *Carrie* begin with different letters but with the same sound.

Extension: To increase the difficulty of this activity, have students group themselves according to the ending sounds in their names.

What Do You Hear?
Standard: 5.1

1. Ask students to listen for sounds they hear at the end of words.

2. Begin by saying a single word, such as *dog*. Ask the students, "What sound do you hear at the end of *dog*?"

3. Emphasize the sound as you say it for students who need assistance.

4. Continue this activity by saying two or three words with the same ending sound, such as *mat*, *bat*, and, *hit*. "What sound do you hear at the end of these words?" See below for groups of words to use for practice.

Words ending with /b/ sound

- grab
- sob
- rub
- bib

Words ending with /m/ sound

- hum
- mom
- time
- game

Words ending with /l/ sound

- doll
- school
- fell
- drill

Words ending with /r/ sound

- car
- tear
- store
- roar

Words ending with /s/ sound

- kiss
- house
- case
- bass

Words ending with /d/ sound

- had
- kid
- toad
- said

Phoneme-Isolation Activities *(cont.)*

Picture Sounds

Standard: 5.1

This activity assists your students with identification of sounds in words.

Materials

- picture cards (below and on pages 10–12)
- crayons and markers (optional)
- scissors

1. Duplicate the cards below and on pages 10–12. Color and laminate the cards, if desired, and cut them apart.

2. Show the students how to use the cards. A student selects a card from the stack and says the name of the picture.

3. Ask the student questions, such as the following:

   ➤ What sound do you hear at the beginning of the word?

   ➤ What sound do you hear at the end of the word?

   ➤ Can you think of another word that begins with the same sound?

   ➤ Can you think of another word that ends with the same sound?

Continue in this manner, giving all students the opportunity to participate. Place the cards in a learning center and encourage the students to continue to practice on their own or with partners.

Picture Cards

See pages 10–12 for more picture cards.

Picture Cards

Picture Cards *(cont.)*

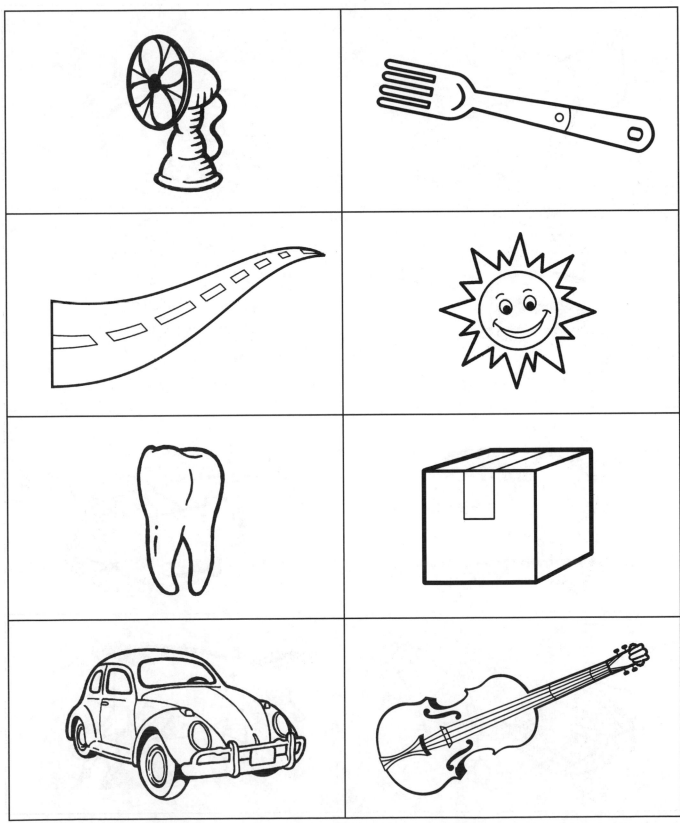

Picture Cards *(cont.)*

Phoneme-Identity Activities

Phoneme identity is the ability to recognize that some words contain the same sounds.

Sound Detectives

Standard: 5.1

1. Gather students together. Explain that you will say three words. Their job is to determine which sound is the same in each word.

2. Begin by saying three words with the same beginning sound—such as *ball*, *baby*, and *bit*. After students identify that each word has the /b/ sound, ask them which word contains that sound more than once. (*baby*)

3. Try this with several groups of words with the same beginning sound.

4. Make the activity more challenging by saying groups of words with the same ending sound, middle sound, or a combination of these. See below for groups of words.

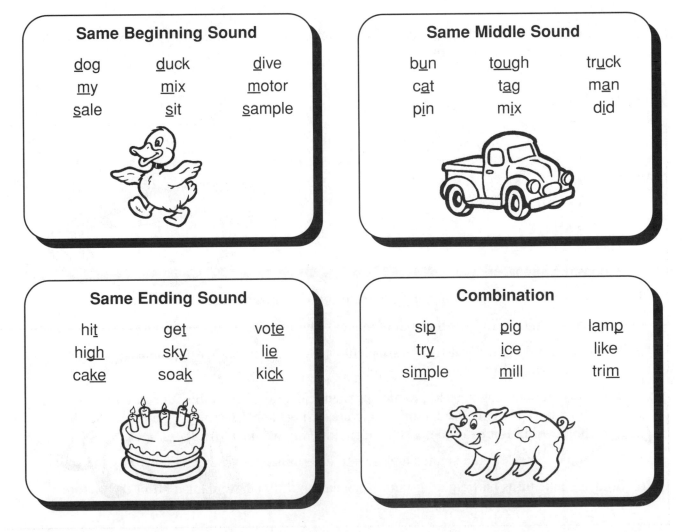

Same Beginning Sound

<u>d</u>og	<u>d</u>uck	<u>d</u>ive
<u>m</u>y	<u>m</u>ix	<u>m</u>otor
<u>s</u>ale	<u>s</u>it	<u>s</u>ample

Same Middle Sound

b<u>u</u>n	t<u>ou</u>gh	tr<u>u</u>ck
c<u>a</u>t	t<u>a</u>g	m<u>a</u>n
p<u>i</u>n	m<u>i</u>x	d<u>i</u>d

Same Ending Sound

hi<u>t</u>	ge<u>t</u>	vo<u>te</u>
hig<u>h</u>	sk<u>y</u>	li<u>e</u>
ca<u>ke</u>	soa<u>k</u>	ki<u>ck</u>

Combination

si<u>p</u>	<u>p</u>ig	lam<u>p</u>
tr<u>y</u>	<u>i</u>ce	l<u>i</u>ke
si<u>m</u>ple	<u>m</u>ill	tri<u>m</u>

Phoneme-Identity Activities *(cont.)*

What Do You Hear?

Standard: 5.1

Use this activity to encourage students to listen to the sounds in words.

Materials

- index cards
- markers
- paper lunch bag

1. Write each letter of the alphabet on a different index card.

2. Place the cards in a bag. In turn, invite each student to reach in the bag and select a card.

3. Have each child think of three words that contain that sound.

4. Ask each student to say the three words and have classmates try to determine the sound that is the same in each word.

5. You may want to conduct this activity with small groups of children as a daily activity, with five different children participating each day.

Picture This!

Standard: 5.1

Here's a fun way to practice identification of phonemes.

Materials

- old magazines
- scissors
- glue
- construction paper

1. Begin by providing each student with one or two old magazines.

2. Instruct the student to look through the magazine to find and cut out pictures he or she likes.

3. When the child has cut out five or six pictures, instruct him or her to glue each picture onto a sheet of construction paper.

4. Then pair students together to practice phoneme identity. To do this, the children take turns. The first child says the name of one of the pictures using each separate phoneme, rather than saying the whole word. For example, a student saying *lady* would say /l/ /a/ /d/ /ee/.

5. The partner listens to the sounds and tries to determine the word represented by the sounds.

6. Students take turns participating in this manner until they have named all of the pictures.

Phoneme-Categorization Activities

Phoneme categorization is the ability to recognize words that sound the same or different.

Which Word Doesn't Belong?

Standard: 5.1

1. For this activity, your students will be asked to identify one word in a set of three that does not sound the same as the others.

2. Say the words *bun*, *fun*, and *cake*. Ask the students to identify which word doesn't belong.

3. Ask the students to explain why the word is different. Try this activity with rhyming words as well as with words that have same and different beginning and ending sounds.

4. To make the activity more challenging, have your students listen for similar and different blends. Here are some sample word groups:

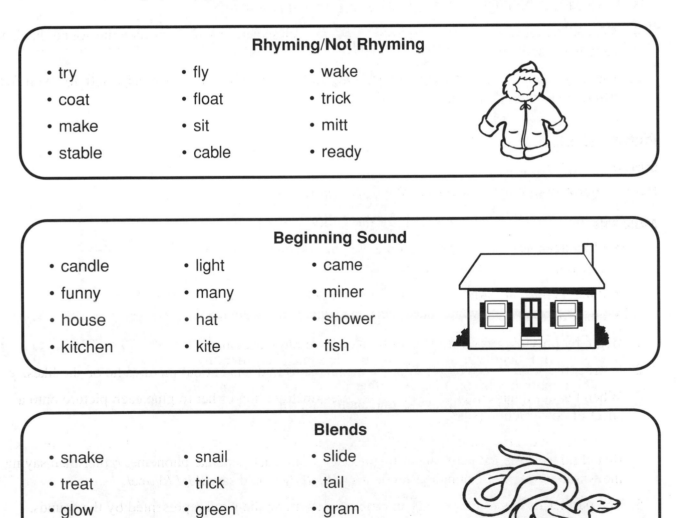

Rhyming/Not Rhyming

- try
- coat
- make
- stable

- fly
- float
- sit
- cable

- wake
- trick
- mitt
- ready

Beginning Sound

- candle
- funny
- house
- kitchen

- light
- many
- hat
- kite

- came
- miner
- shower
- fish

Blends

- snake
- treat
- glow
- brow

- snail
- trick
- green
- brick

- slide
- tail
- gram
- blow

Phoneme-Categorization Activities *(cont.)*

Same Middle Sound

Standard: 5.1

This activity will assist your students in identifying words that sound the same or different.

1. Similar to the activity on page 15, students are asked to identify the word in a set that does not sound the same as the others. In this game, however, have students listen for words with the same middle sounds.

2. Say three words with the same sound and one with a different sound—for example, *lap, man, cot,* and *ran*.

3. Ask the students to explain how the word is different.

Sound Categorization

Standard: 5.1

This learning-center activity provides your students with ongoing practice of categorizing sounds in words.

Materials

- cards on pages 17–19
- scissors
- resealable plastic bags

1. Duplicate the cards on pages 17–19 and cut them out.

2. Color the cards and laminate them for durability.

3. Place each set of three cards in a resealable plastic bag and place the bags at a learning center.

4. To play, a child takes the cards out of a bag, reads the words, and determines which words have the same sounds and which word is different.

5. Have the child identify how the words are the same and different.

6. The child continues in this manner with each set of words. Encourage children to work together to assess one another's progress.

funny

bunny

Categorization Cards

strong	**wrong**	**ring**
trip	**flip**	**map**
funny	**bunny**	**chilly**
chair	**hair**	**far**

Categorization Cards *(cont.)*

roar	rage	gain
cloud	clay	cry
fan	run	game
brush	trash	crutch

Categorization Cards *(cont.)*

share	shy	slow
strike	shell	string
nip	slip	snap
met	mask	nest

Phoneme-Blending Activities

Phoneme blending is the ability to combine spoken phonemes into words.

Sound Riddles

Standard: 5.1

Play a sound blending game with your students.

1. Think of a word and say the separate sounds that make up the word—for example, /t/ /r/ /u/ and /k/ for *truck*.

2. The students listen to the sounds and combine them to make the word *truck*.

3. Begin by using shorter words and increase the difficulty with longer words. (See the lists below.)

4. Allow the students to think of their own words to share with the class in the same manner.

One-Syllable Words		
track	→	/t/ /r/ /a/ /k/
dog	→	/d/ /o/ /g/
cup	→	/c/ /u/ /p/
pill	→	/p/ /i/ /l/
brush	→	/b/ /r/ /u/ /sh/

Two-Syllable Words		
carpet	→	/c/ /a/ /r/ /p/ /e/ /t/
table	→	/t/ /a/ /b/ /l/
desert	→	/d/ /e/ /s/ /r/ /t/
closet	→	/c/ /l/ /o/ /s/ /e/ /t/
baseball	→	/b/ /a/ /s/ /b/ /a/ /l/

Listen to the Sounds

Standard: 5.1

This activity will help your students blend sounds together.

1. Just as you have done in the activity above, invite students to select their own words.

2. After each student thinks of a word, have him or her say the word slowly to determine the individual sounds.

3. Invite each student, in turn, to say each sound in the word as classmates try to guess the word.

Phoneme-Segmentation Activities

Phoneme segmentation is the ability to break words into their separate phonemes.

Sound Clapping

Standard: 5.1

1. For this activity, ask the students to listen to the segments or syllables of sounds they hear in words.

2. Say a word and have the students clap the syllables. For example, *kite* has one clap (or syllable) and *hospital* has three.

3. To make the activity more challenging, have the children listen to a word, think about the number of syllables, and then clap the syllables to check their answers.

Tracking Sounds

Standard: 5.1

Using this activity will help your students to identify the number of sounds in a word.

Materials

- copy of page 22 (laminated) for each student
- wipe-off markers

1. Prepare for the activity by duplicating and laminating the chart on page 22 for each student. Provide each child with a wipe-off marker.

2. To play, the teacher says a word and has each child think of the number of individual sounds he or she can hear in the word.

3. The child makes an **X** for each sound heard. For example, the child would mark **XXXX** for the word *glass* (/g/ /l/ /a/ /s/).

4. After completing this for each word, show the children the actual spelling of the word and discuss the fact that not all letters in a word are represented by separate sounds.

5. To use this as a learning center activity, make a tape recording of your voice slowly pronouncing a series of words.

6. Students listen to the words on the tape recording and mark on the chart the number of sounds they hear.

Tracking Sounds

Directions: Say or listen to a word. Draw an **X** to represent each sound you hear in the word.

1.					
2.					
3.					
4.					
5.					
6.					

Phoneme-Segmentation Activities *(cont.)*

Sound Spelling

Standard: 5.1

This activity will help your children to transfer the identification of sounds to spelling the words in writing.

Materials

- chart paper
- marker
- paper
- pencils

1. This activity will likely not be necessary for all of your second-graders, but you may find that a few of your students will benefit from it.

2. Gather these students together and provide each with paper and pencil.

3. Say a word and discuss the individual sounds they hear in the word.

4. Demonstrate on chart paper how the word can be written phonetically based on the sounds they hear.

5. Instruct the students to try this on their own. Be sure to assist those who are experiencing difficulties.

6. Helping your students to use invented spelling will assist them in writing independently, which will lead to increased ability to spell conventionally over time.

Spelling Assistance

When assisting children with spelling words, we often say things, such as:

- "Sound it out."
- "What sound do you hear next?"

The problem with this is that some children have difficulty with phoneme segmentation. Rather than asking, "What sound do you hear?" it can be more helpful to say the next sound and ask the child what letter represents the sound. See the scenario below.

Child: How do you spell *dog*?

Teacher: Let's listen to the sounds in *dog*. The first sound says /d/. What letter makes the /d/ sound?

Child: D!

Teacher: Good! Write that down. Now let's listen to the next sound in *dog*.

Working with a child in this manner will help him or her become aware of individual sounds while writing independently.

Phoneme-Deletion Activities

Phoneme deletion is identifying a new word when a phoneme is removed from another word.

What's Left?

Standard: 5.1

This activity encourages your students to be sound detectives.

1. Say a word and then ask the children to determine what the word would change to if a sound is removed—for example, "What word is left if we remove the /s/ from *smile*?" (*mile*)

2. Continue in this manner. A list of these riddles is provided below.

   • What word is left if we remove the /t/ in *trust*? (**rust**)

   • What word is left if we remove the /c/ in *cable*? (**able**)

   • What word is left if we remove the /t/ in *plant*? (**plan**)

   • What word is left if we remove the /n/ in *snake*? (**sake**)

   • What word is left if we remove the /d/ in *board*? (**boar**)

   • What word is left if we remove the /c/ in *cat*? (**at**)

   • What word is left if we remove the /n/ in *brown*? (**brow**)

   • What word is left if we remove the /p/ in *plate*? (**late**)

   • What word is left if we remove the /l/ in *slick*? (**sick**)

Deletion Cards

Standard: 5.1

Use this activity to allow your children to practice phoneme deletion independently.

Materials: copies of cards on pages 25 and 26, scissors

1. Duplicate the word cards on pages 25 and 26. Laminate the cards and cut them apart.

2. You will notice that each card has one or two dots below the word. The dots indicate places where the card can be folded backward to delete a letter.

3. The student's job is to read the original word and then determine the word that will remain when the first or last letter is removed. Here is an example:

Deletion Cards

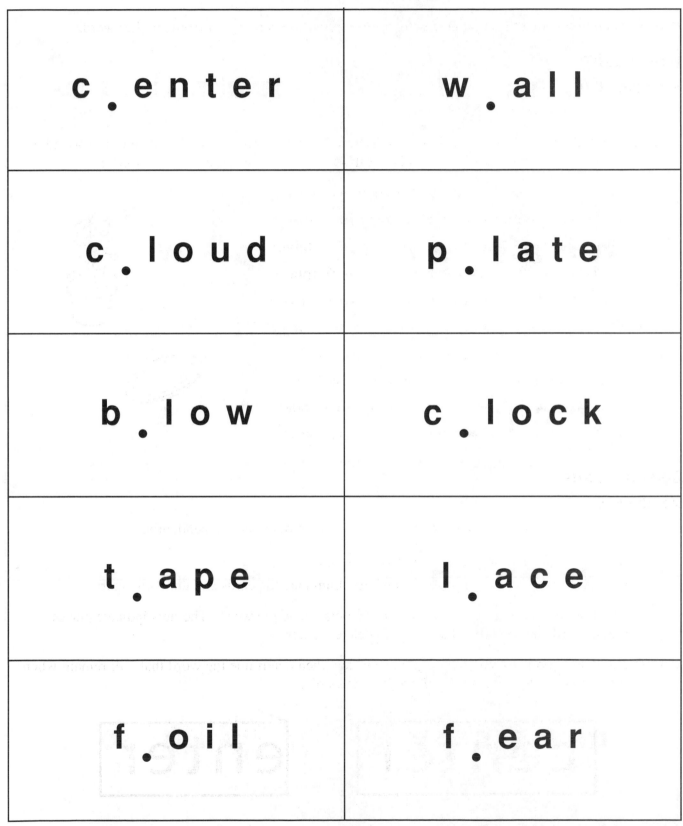

c.enter	w.all
c.loud	p.late
b.low	c.lock
t.ape	l.ace
f.oil	f.ear

Deletion Cards *(cont.)*

c a r **.** d	h a n d **.** l e
h e a t **.** e r	p a w **.** n
c o p **.** y	b u s **.** t
b a n **.** d	l a w **.** n
m e s s **.** y	w i n **.** d

Phoneme Addition & Substitution Activities

Phoneme addition and substitution involves changing a phoneme in a word to make a new word.

Making New Words

Standard: 5.1

Your children will determine the creation of new words with this activity.

1. To play, say a word. Then ask how the word would change if a particular sound were added. For example, "Listen to the word *flee*. What word do we have if we add /t/ at the end?" (*fleet*)

2. Continue in this manner with the words listed below. Allow the children to create some of their own phonemic additions.

• pin /ch/	• clam /p/	• /a/ cross
• wind /y/	• gas /p/	• /s/ car
• plan /t/	• fir /st/	• /t/ rip

Presto Change-o!

Standard: 5.1

Similar to the activity above, the children determine how a word changes when one sound is replaced with another.

1. To play, say a word. Then ask how the word would change if a particular sound were substituted for another. For example, "Listen to the word *trip*. What word would we have if we changed the /p/ to /m/?" (*trim*)

2. Continue in this manner with the words listed below. Allow the children to create some of their own phonemic substitutions.

• dog/log

• pit/pin

• cat/can

• tale/tame

• leather/weather

• dinner/winner

• paper/pager

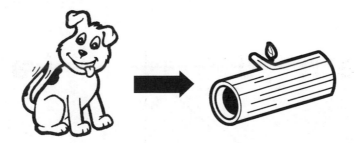

Phoneme Riddles

What happens when you change a sound in a word to another sound? Answer each riddle below.

1. Change the /t/ in **cut** to /p/. What is the new word? _____

2. Change the first /g/ in **giggle** to /w/. What is the new word? _____

3. Change the /m/ in **middle** to /r/. What is the new word? _____

4. Change the /t/ in **chat** to /p/. What is the new word? _____

5. Change the /m/ in **milk** to /s/. What is the new word? _____

6. Change the /u/ in **rug** to /a/. What is the new word? _____

7. Change the /p/ in **picket** to /t/. What is the new word? _____

8. Change the /r/ in **rake** to /c/. What is the new word? _____

9. Change the /b/ in **bow** to /l/. What is the new word? _____

10. Change the /c/ in **crown** to /b/. What is the new word? _____

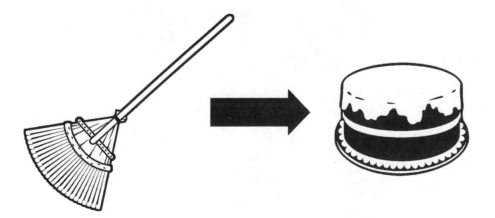

4-Point Rubric

Use this rubric to assist in assessing students' progress with phonemic awareness.

Points	Description
4	The student understands that words are made up of individual sounds. The student consistently identifies the sounds in words, blends sounds together, adds and substitutes sounds to make new words, etc.
3	The student understands that words are made up of individual sounds. The student is often able to identify the sounds in words, blend sounds together, add and substitute sounds to make new words, etc.
2	The student is beginning to understand that words are made up of individual sounds. The student inconsistently identifies the sounds in words, blends sounds together, adds and substitutes sounds to make new words, etc.
1	The student struggles with the understanding that words are made up of individual sounds.

Assessment

Create your own six-point rubric to assess your students' phonemic awareness. For each section of the rubric, determine the necessary criteria. For example, number 6 might read, "The student has a thorough understanding of all areas of phonemic awareness." Number 1 might read, "The student struggles with the identification of sounds."

Points	Description
6	
5	
4	
3	
2	
1	

Assessment *(cont.)*

Student's Name: _____

Skill	Mastery	Improving	Struggling
Phoneme Isolation			
Phoneme Identity			
Phoneme Categorization			
Phoneme Blending			
Phoneme Segmentation			
Phoneme Deletion			
Phoneme Addition			
Phoneme Substitution			

See page 32 for descriptions of each assessment level.

Assessment Descriptions

Use the descriptions below to assist you in completing the assessment chart on page 31.

Observe students as they perform various phonemic awareness activities.

✐ Mastery

A student has achieved mastery when he or she demonstrates 80% accuracy or better in the phonemic awareness areas listed at the bottom of the page.

✐ Improving

A student is classified as improving when he or she demonstrates 60% accuracy or better in the phonemic awareness areas listed at the bottom of the page.

✐ Struggling

A student is classified as struggling when he or she demonstrates less than 60% accuracy in the phonemic awareness areas listed at the bottom of the page.

Phonemic-Awareness Descriptions

- Phoneme Isolation = recognizing sounds in words

- Phoneme Identity = recognizing words that have similar sounds

- Phoneme Categorization = recognizing words that sound the same and words that sound different

- Phoneme Blending = combining spoken phonemes into words

- Phoneme Segmentation = breaking words into their separate phonemes

- Phoneme Deletion = identifying a new word when a phoneme is removed from another word

- Phoneme Addition = identifying a new word when a phoneme is added to another word

- Phoneme Substitution = changing a phoneme in a word to make a new word

Phonics

As a result of the debate between phonics and whole-language, phonics instruction has become a controversial issue with many educators. It is important to keep in mind that phonics instruction is not intended to be the sole method of reading instruction. Phonics skills do, however, help children learn the relationships between the letters of written language and the sounds of spoken language. This leads to an understanding of the alphabetic principle.

Why Teach Phonics?

Phonics instruction is important because it improves:

- children's word recognition and spelling in kindergarten and first grade
- reading comprehension
- the skills of children with reading difficulties

In order for phonics instruction to be most effective, it should be introduced early on. Phonics instruction in this area is typically only necessary through the second grade; and it should not be the entire focus of a reading program, but rather an important part of a well-balanced program.

As described in the report of The National Reading Panel, there are several approaches to phonics instruction—synthetic phonics, analytic phonics, analogy-based phonics, phonics through spelling, embedded phonics, and onset-rime instruction. Some educators use one approach exclusively, while others used a combination of approaches. These approaches are described here:

- ➤ **Synthetic Phonics**—Children learn to convert letters into sounds, blending the sounds together to form recognizable words.

- ➤ **Analytic Phonics**—Children analyze letter-sound relationships in words they have already learned. Sounds are not taught or pronounced in isolation.

- ➤ **Analogy-based Phonics**—Children identify new words by using what they know about parts of word families.

- ➤ **Phonics through Spelling**—Children break words into individual sounds and write words by identifying each phoneme and writing a letter to represent it.

- ➤ **Embedded Phonics**—Children are taught letter/sound relationships in the context of reading.

- ➤ **Onset-Rime Instruction**—Children identify the sound of the letter(s) before the onset (or first vowel) in a one-syllable word and the sound of the rime (or the renaming part of the word).

In this section of the book, you will find activities related to the above methods of phonics teaching. These activities will address the following phonics topics:

- long and short vowels
- double vowels
- irregular double vowels
- "r"-controlled vowels
- "y" as a vowel
- silent "e"
- hard and soft "c" and "g"
- compound words
- "-ing" endings
- contractions
- plurals
- blends
- digraphs
- diphthongs

Word Families

Word Family Chains

Standard: 5.5

Materials

- chart paper
- markers
- construction paper
- scissors
- glue, tape, or stapler

1. Choose a word family (see below) and ask students to think of as many words as possible that contain that word ending.

2. Write these words on chart paper to assist the children.

3. Show the students how to cut several construction-paper strips and write a different word from the chart on each strip.

4. Next, use the strips to make a paper chain. (You can glue, tape, or staple the chain links together.)

5. After making one word family chain as a class, instruct each student to make one of his or her own.

6. The student should select a different word family, make a list of words, and then use the words to make a paper chain. Here is a list of word families to choose from:

Word Families			
ack	ash	eep	ing
ad	at	en	og
ail	ain	ell	oil
all	ake	ent	ood
am	ate	est	out
ame	aw	ice	own
an	ay	ill	ug
ap	eel	in	ump

Vowel Activities

Use these activities to provide your students with a solid understanding of long and short vowels.

Short Vowels

Standard: 5.5

This activity provides practice for identifying short vowel sounds.

Materials

- small magazine pictures with different middle vowel sounds
- five small envelopes
- marker

1. Cut out an assortment of magazine pictures. It is best if the pictures represent one-syllable words. Cut out pictures representing short *a* (cat, pan, cab), short *e* (hen, pen), short *i* (hill, pin), short *o* (pot, stop sign), short *u* (cup, rug). Laminate the pictures for durability.
2. Next, label each of the five envelopes with a different vowel (short *a*, short *e*, short *i*, short *o*, short *u*).
3. To play, a student determines the name of each picture and the short vowel sound heard. The child places each picture inside the correct envelope.

Long or Short?

Standard: 5.5

This activity provides your students with practice identifying short and long vowel sounds.

Materials

- copies of pages 36–40
- scissors
- pencils
- crayons or markers (optional)
- manila envelope

1. Duplicate page 36–40 and cut the cards apart.
2. Using a pencil, write the word *long* or *short* on the back of each scoop for self-checking.
3. Color and laminate the cards, if desired.
4. Place the cards in a manila envelope for storage.
5. To play, a student places the "Long Vowel" and "Short Vowel" cones on a desktop.
6. The child then reads each word on an ice-cream scoop and determines whether the vowel sound is long or short.
7. The child then stacks the scoop above the correct cone.
8. The child checks his or her own work by looking on the backs of the ice-cream scoops.

Long and Short Vowels

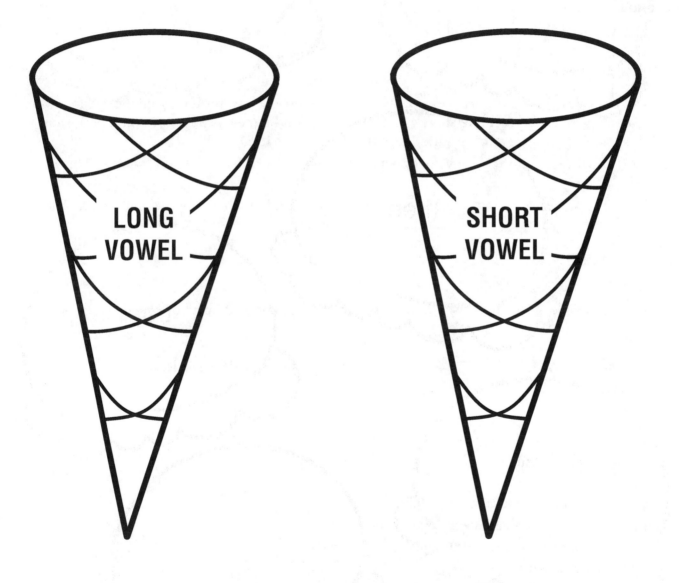

Long and Short Vowels *(cont.)*

hat

sick

men

trap

pest

set

Long and Short Vowels *(cont.)*

Long and Short Vowels *(cont.)*

Long and Short Vowels *(cont.)*

hope

soap

go

glue

fuse

tube

Double-Vowels Activities

"ai" Versus "ay"

Standard: 5.5

The long *a* sound can be made with the letters *ai* and *ay*. Explain to your students that *ai* usually comes in the middle of a word (such as *rain*) and *ay* usually comes at the end of a word (such as *hay*).

"ee" Versus "ea"

Standard: 5.5

Understanding when to use *ee* or *ea* for the long *e* sound is difficult, but it will get easier for the children the more opportunities they have to encounter these words. When reading stories that contain words with *ee* and *ea*, be sure to draw attention to them and review their use to represent the long *e* sound. Provide some practice with reading words containing *ee* and *ea* by having each student complete page 42.

"ie" and "oe"

Standard: 5.5

Sometimes when two vowels are together at the end of a one-syllable word, a long sound can be heard. One-syllable words that end in *ie* make the long *i* sound, such as *pie* and *lie*. One-syllable words that end in *oe* make the long *o* sound, such as *hoe* and *toe*. As a group activity, ask your students to think of as many one-syllable words as possible that end in *oe* or *ie*. Evaluate whether the words end with long *o* or long *i*. See the list below.

"oe" Words	"ie" Words
foe	die
hoe	lie
Joe	pie
toe	tie
woe	

Words with "ee" and "ea"

Circle the word that names each picture.

leak lean least	seal sleep seem	beats beads beans
jeans jeep treat	meal meat meet	seeds seek seat
treat tree tear	wheel we wear	fear feet feel

Phonics Activities

The activities below correspond to reproducibles on pages 44–50.

"y" as a Vowel

Standard: 5.5

Review with the children that the letter *y* sometimes makes a long *e* or long *i* sound. Ask the students to name words they can think of where *y* makes a vowel sound. Record these words on chart paper. Duplicate page 44 for each student. To complete the page, a student writes a word that corresponds with each picture. Each word should have *y* used as a vowel.

Silent "e"

Standard: 5.5

For this activity, review with the children that when *e* is added to the end of some words, the vowel in the word changes to a long sound. For example, if *e* is added to the end of *ton, mat,* and *mad,* the words become *tone, mate,* and *made.* Duplicate page 45 for each student for further practice.

Hard and Soft "c" and "g"

Standard: 5.5

Pages 46 and 47 give your students practice with identifying the hard and soft sounds of *c* and *g.* Review the following rules with the students before they complete the page.
- When *c* is followed by *a, o,* or *u,* it usually makes a hard sound.
- When *c* is followed by *e, i,* or *y,* it usually makes a soft sound.
- When *g* is followed by *a, i, o,* or *u,* it usually makes a hard sound.
- When *g* is followed by *e* or *y,* it usually makes a soft sound.

Compound Words

Standard: 5.6

Explain to your students that when two words are put together to make another word, we call it a compound word. For example, *sun* and *shine* make the word *sunshine.* Duplicate page 48 and have the students solve each picture riddle by putting two words together to make a new word.

Contractions

Standard: 5.6

Your students will enjoy practicing contractions with this activity. Duplicate and cut apart the cards on pages 49 and 50. Fold each card forward on the dotted line. On the back of each fold, write a different contraction part. For example, on the back of the fold for *she is,* write *'s.* When the card is folded, the words *she is* become the contraction *she's.* Here are the contraction parts to write on the backs of the folds:

do not—*'t*	could not—*n't*	who is—*'s*	we have—*'ve*
cannot—*'t*	should not—*n't*	there is—*'s*	you will—*'ll*
have not—*n't*	she is—*'s*	they are—*'re*	he will—*'ll*
will not—*on't*	he is—*'s*	we are—*'re*	she will—*'ll*
would not—*n't*	it is—*'s*	they have—*'ve*	they will—*'ll*

"y" as a Vowel

Directions: Sometimes the letter *y* acts as a vowel in a word. Sometimes the *y* makes a long *i* sound. Sometime the *y* makes a long *e* sound. Each picture below is of a word that has a *y* in it. Write the word below each picture.

On the lines below, write three more words with **y** as a vowel.

_____   _____   _____

Silent "e"

Directions: Add an *e* to the end of each group of letters. Write a sentence using each word.

1. can ☐

_____

_____

2. plan ☐

_____

_____

3. fin ☐

_____

_____

4. kit ☐

_____

_____

5. dim ☐

_____

_____

6. tun ☐

_____

_____

7. tim ☐

_____

_____

8. ston ☐

_____

Hard and Soft "g"

Directions: When *g* is followed by *a*, *i*, *o*, or *u*, it usually makes a hard sound as in *gift*. When g is followed by *e* or *y*, it usually makes a soft sound, as in *gentle*. Write *hard* or *soft* beside each word. The first one has been done for you.

1. gorilla _____ | hard |
2. gym _____ | |
3. guess _____ | |
4. gas _____ | |
5. gem _____ | |
6. gum _____ | |
7. gill _____ | |
8. got _____ | |
9. gentleman _____ | |
10. go _____ | |
11. gone _____ | |
12. guts _____ | |
13. gypsy _____ | |
14. gap _____ | |

Hard and Soft "c"

Directions: When *c* is followed by *a*, *o*, or *u*, it usually makes a hard sound as in *candy*. When *c* is followed by *e*, *i*, or *y*, it usually makes a soft sound as in *cent*. Write *hard* or *soft* beside each word.

1. cent _

2. candy _

3. cycle _

4. cell _

5. cob _

6. cite _

7. cub _

8. cut _

9. can _

10. cover _

11. center _

12. comb _

13. cellar _

14. candle _

Compound Words

Directions: Solve each riddle by writing a compound word on the line.

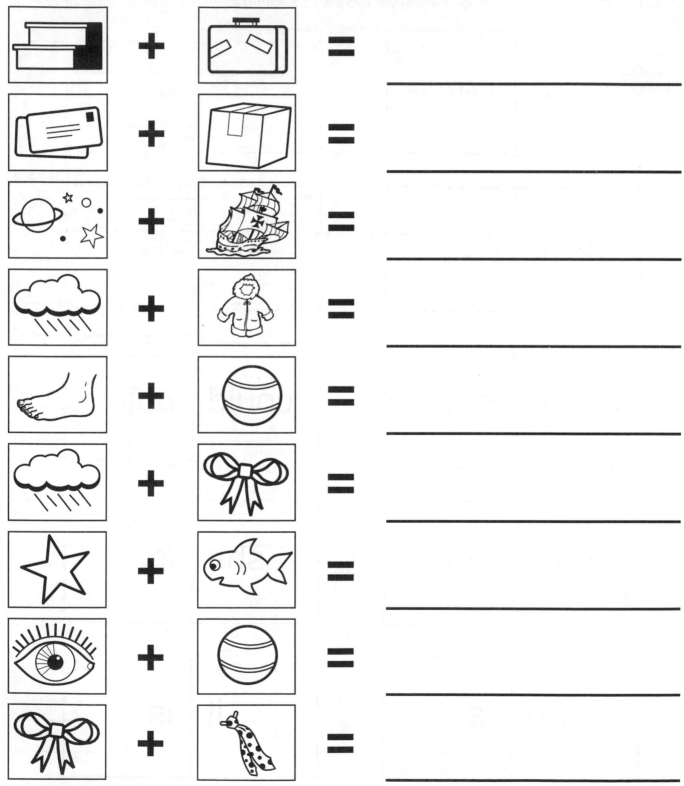

Contractions

Directions: Duplicate and cut out the cards. Fold each card on the dotted line. On the back of the fold, write the word part to make a contraction. See page 43 for further directions.

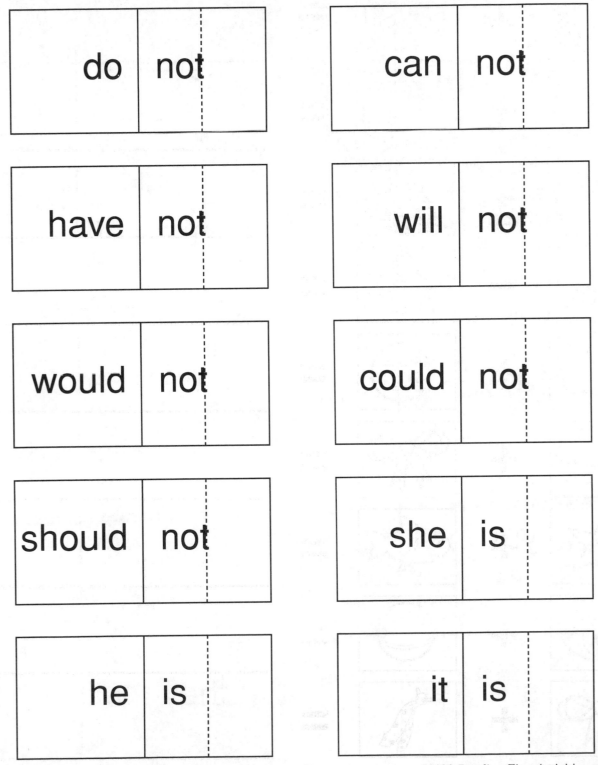

Contractions *(cont.)*

Directions: Duplicate and cut out the cards. Fold each card on the dotted line. On the back of the fold, write the word part to make a contraction. See page 43 for further directions.

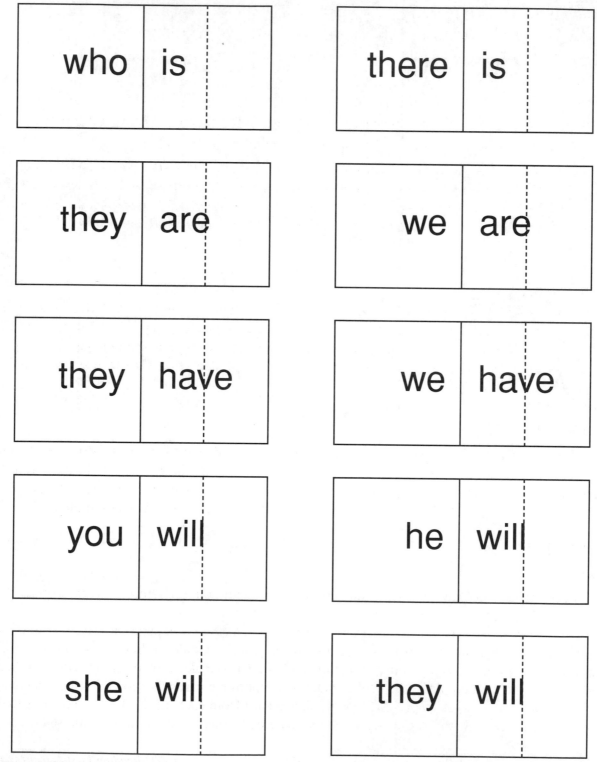

who	is		there	is
they	are		we	are
they	have		we	have
you	will		he	will
she	will		they	will

More Phonics Activities

The activities below correspond to reproducibles on pages 52–61.

"-ing" Endings

Standard: 5.6

This game will help students understand these rules for adding *ing* to words:

- When a short-vowel word ends in a single consonant, double the vowel before adding *ing*. (**tap** → **tapping**)
- When a long-vowel word ends in a single consonant, just add *ing*. (**train** → **training**)
- When a word ends in two consonants, just add *ing*. (**sell** → **selling**; **jump** → **jumping**)
- When a word ends in silent *e*, drop the *e* and add *ing*. (**time** → **timing**)

To prepare for the game, duplicate the cards on pages 52 and 53. Cut them apart. Two children spread out the word cards face up; the rule cards are stacked facedown. In turn, the students select a rule card and then look for a word that follows the rule. If the student is correct, he or she keeps the word card. If incorrect, the student puts the card back. The student with the most word cards wins.

Plurals

Standard: 5.6

Pages 54 and 55 will assist your children in learning to make words plural. Page 54 focuses on adding *s* or *es* using this rule: if a word ends in *s*, *ss*, *x*, *z*, *sh*, or *ch*, add *es*, otherwise just add *s*. Page 55 focuses on changing *y* to *i* before adding *es*. Review these rules with your students before completing the pages. Display examples of these words in use and have students come up with a few of their own.

Blends Puzzle

Standard: 5.5

To help your students practice making blends, duplicate pages 56 and 57 onto cardstock. Cut apart the puzzle pieces and laminate them. Place each puzzle in a resealable plastic bag for storage. To play, a child assembles the puzzle pieces by making blend words. Some blends can be used with many word ends, so students will need to find the exact placement of each piece to assemble the puzzles.

Diphthongs

Standard: 5.5

Pages 58–61 provide the materials for a fun activity using diphthongs. Before playing, explain that diphthongs make "sliding" sounds when two letters are put together, such as *ow* in *cow* or *oy* in *boy*. Review other diphthongs. Duplicate pages 59 and 60 and laminate. On page 58, carefully cut a slit on each dotted line. Cut apart the cards on page 59. To play, a child slides a diphthong card into each slit to form a word. For additional practice, use pages 60 and 61 to make another game with diphthongs. Duplicate, laminate, and cut apart the cards. Stack the diphthong cards facedown in one stack and the letter cards in another stack. To play, a student takes a card from each stack. If the two cards make a word, the student keeps them. If they don't, the cards are returned to the bottom of the stacks.

"-ing" Endings

See the directions on page 51.

Rule Card	Rule Card	Rule Card
Drop the *e* and add *ing*.	Double the consonant and add *ing*.	Just add *ing*.
Rule Card	**Rule Card**	**Rule Card**
Drop the *e* and add *ing*.	Double the consonant and add *ing*.	Just add *ing*.
Rule Card	**Rule Card**	**Rule Card**
Drop the *e* and add *ing*.	Double the consonant and add *ing*.	Just add *ing*.

"-ing" Endings *(cont)*

See the directions on page 51.

trip	map	tan
skip	run	yell
help	jump	track
fill	rain	sway
feel	come	bike
change	make	take

Plurals

Directions: Rewrite each word in its plural form by writing *s* or *es* at the end. Use the rule below.

> **Rule:** If a word ends in *s*, *ss*, *x*, *z*, *sh*, or *ch*, add *es*. Otherwise, just add *s*.

1. box _____

2. dog _____

3. brush _____

4. fox _____

5. house _____

6. bench _____

7. pencil _____

8. buzz _____

9. bus _____

10. shirt _____

11. girl _____

12. glass _____

Plurals *(cont.)*

Directions: When a word ends in *y*, change the *y* to *i* and add *es* in order to make it plural. Cut out the boxes below. Glue them in place to make each word plural. (You'll need to glue the box over the *y*.)

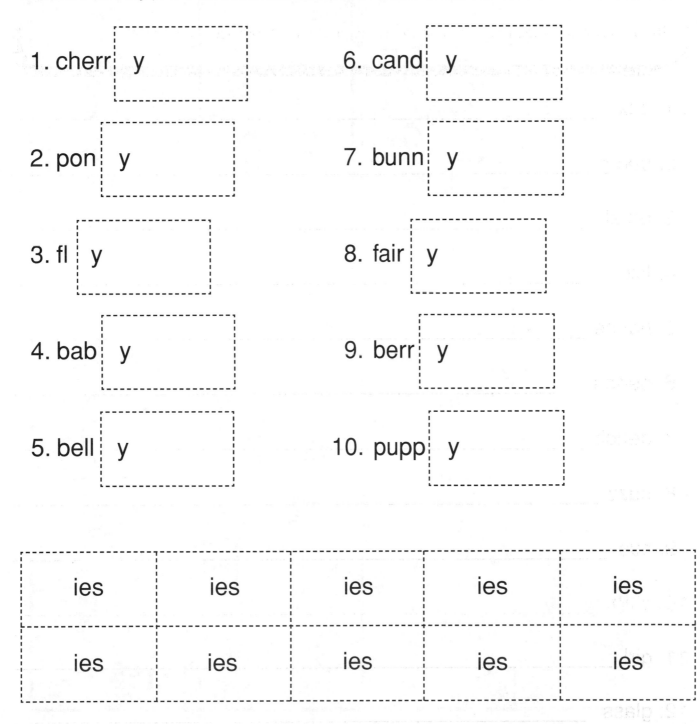

1. cherr | y

2. pon | y

3. fl | y

4. bab | y

5. bell | y

6. cand | y

7. bunn | y

8. fair | y

9. berr | y

10. pupp | y

| ies | ies | ies | ies | ies |
| ies | ies | ies | ies | ies |

Blends Puzzle

See the directions on page 51.

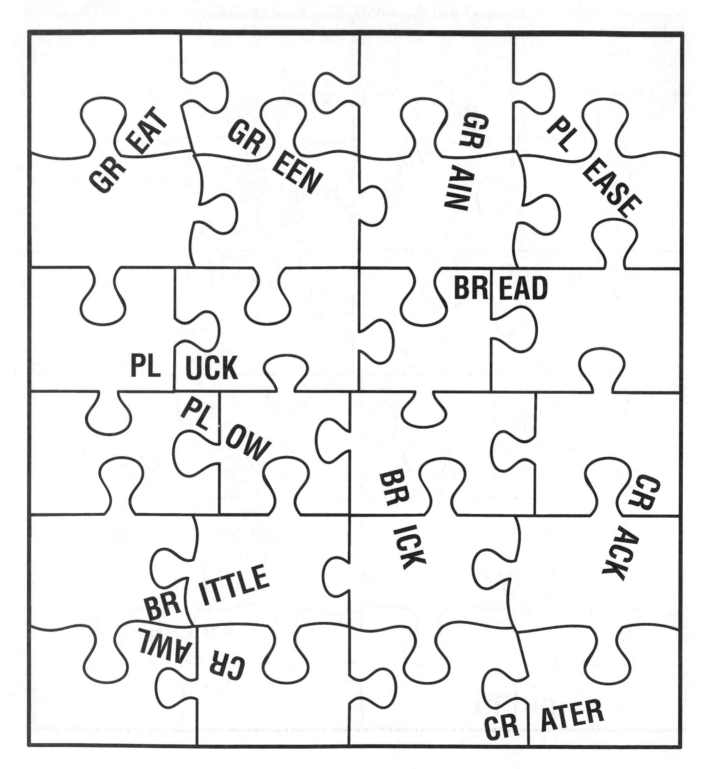

Blends Puzzle *(cont.)*

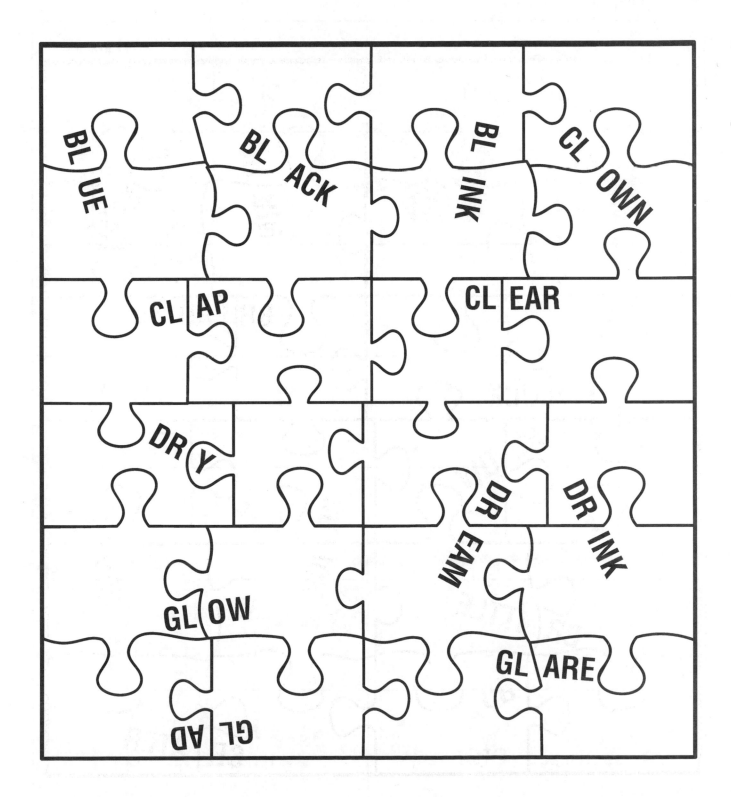

Diphthongs

See the directions on page 51.

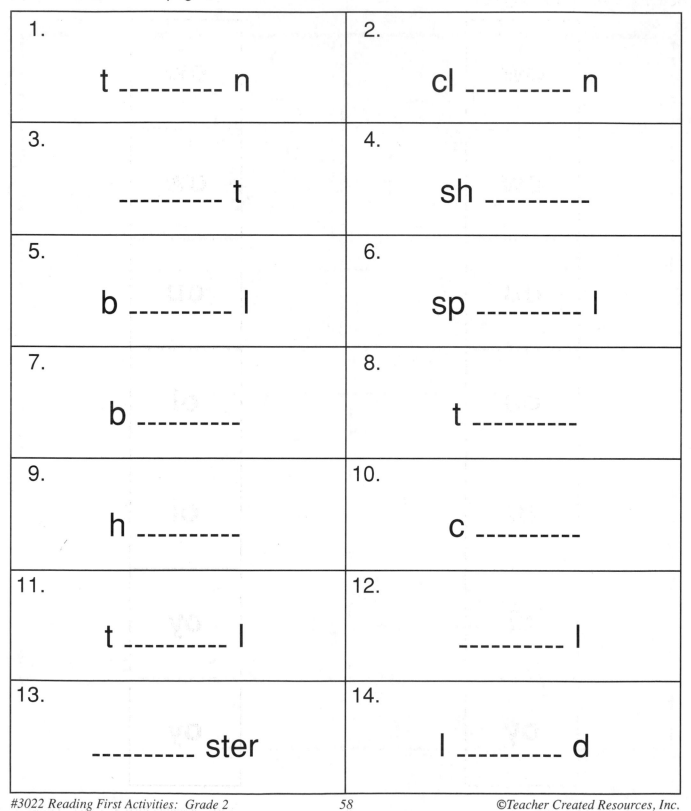

1. t _____ n	2. cl _____ n
3. _____ t	4. sh _____
5. b _____ l	6. sp _____ l
7. b _____	8. t _____
9. h _____	10. c _____
11. t _____ l	12. _____ l
13. _____ ster	14. l _____ d

Diphthongs *(cont.)*

See the directions on page 51.

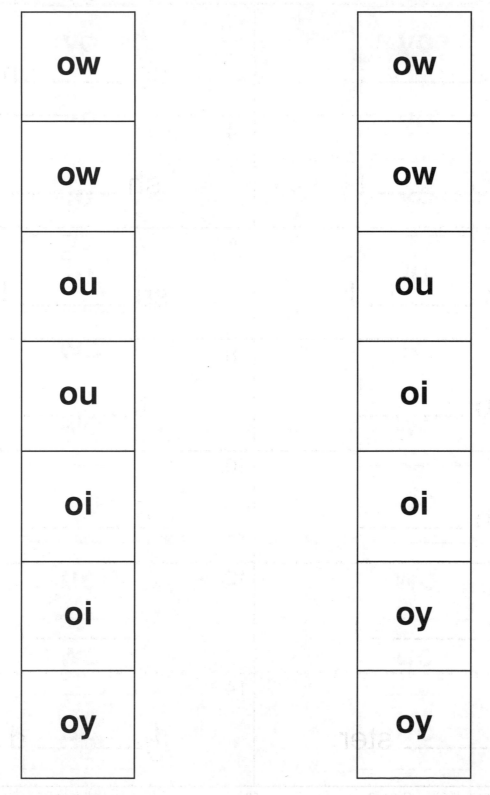

Diphthongs Game

See the directions on page 51.

oy	**oy**
oy	**oy**
oy	**oi**
oi	**oi**
oi	**ow**
ow	**ow**
ow	**ow**
ow	**ou**
ou	**ow**
ou	**ou**

Diphthongs Game *(cont.)*

See the directions on page 51.

h _____	c _____
n _____	y _____
pl _____	t _____
r _____	l _____ d
sh _____ t	r _____ nd
c _____ n	t _____ n
_____ nk	n _____ n
ch _____ ce	j _____
s _____	b _____
t _____	_____ ster

Phonics Assessment Chart

Student Name: _____

Phonics Skill	Date Introduced	Date of Mastery (80% accuracy or better)
word families		
long vowels		
short vowels		
double vowels		
y as a vowel		
silent *e*		
hard and soft *c*		
hard and soft *g*		
compound words		
contractions		
-ing endings		
plurals		
blends		
diphthongs		

Fluency

The term *fluency* refers to a child's ability to read quickly with minimal errors. Fluent readers can:

- recognize words with automaticity
- group words into meaningful chunks
- connect ideas in print to prior knowledge
- draw meaning from print
- read with little effort
- read with expression

Less fluent readers:

- read slowly (or word by word)
- take great effort to read
- focus on decoding
- pay little attention to meaning

When speaking of fluency, you will likely encounter the word *automaticity*. This word is often used interchangeably with *fluency*, which is not entirely accurate. Remember these points:

- ✐ *Automaticity* refers to reading that is quick, effortless, and automatic.
- ✐ *Fluency* involves automaticity, but also refers to reading with expression.

Therefore, a child who reads with fluency reads with automaticity, but a child who reads with automaticity is not necessarily considered to be a fluent reader.

Why Is Fluency Important?

Fluency helps children to move from decoding and word recognition to comprehension. There is a strong correlation between fluency and comprehension, which is why instruction in this area is so important. The reading skills of fluent readers are largely automatic, which allows children to interpret meaning rather than decipher letter sounds and individual words. They are essentially able to see words and automatically comprehend their meaning. Fluency becomes an area of focus after a child learns to break code, which makes it an important focus for second-grade students.

Educators tend to teach fluency in two different ways:

1. **repeated and monitored oral reading**—which involves guidance from a teacher while a child reads a passage aloud several times.
2. **independent silent reading**—which involves many opportunities for students to read silently on their own.

It is believed that repeated and monitored oral reading is the most effective way to assist children with fluency development. Traditional "round-robin" reading, in which children take turns reading aloud, can cause anxiety and only involves the one-time reading of small portions of text. Proper fluency instruction involves the repeated reading of relatively simple passages and the modeling of reading (pauses and expression) by more proficient readers.

This section of the book provides activities in the following areas:

- General Fluency Activities
- Student/Adult Reading
- Choral Reading
- Tape-Assisted Reading
- Partner Reading
- Readers Theater
- Assessment

General Fluency Activities

Read-Alouds

Standard: 5.10

In order for your students to learn to read with fluency, it is important that they hear others read smoothly and with expression.

1. Schedule a time each day to read aloud to your students.

2. Select books with interesting characters and use expressions that correspond to each character's personality.

3. Periodically ask your students questions about the story.

4. Ask them what they think might happen next and have them guess how a character might respond to a future event in the story.

Model and Repeat

Standards: 5.9, 5.10

Students can improve their fluency by practicing and mimicking what they hear.

Materials

- short passages at appropriate levels for students

1. Gather together a small group of students.

2. Provide each student with a short passage of text. (Be sure to select a passage that is at or below the student's independent reading level.)

3. Allow the students to read the passage to become familiar with it.

4. Then model the reading of the first sentence.

5. Ask the students to read the same sentence, using your reading as a model.

6. If the students read in a choppy manner, draw attention to it and ask them to practice reading the sentence smoothly.

7. Continue in the same manner with the remaining sentences in the passage.

8. Then allow each student to read the passage as smoothly as possible.

General Fluency Activities *(cont.)*

What a Character!

Standard: 5.10

This activity will assist your students in identifying the voice of story characters.

1. When reading a story, ask the students to describe one of the characters. Draw attention to the way the character speaks.
   - Does he/she speak loudly?
   - Does he/she react impulsively?
   - Is the character easily angered?
2. Select an event from the story where the character has dialog.
3. Ask the students how the character might say this dialog if he/she is in a different mood (excited, afraid, angry, annoyed, etc.).
4. Draw students' attention to the importance of using expression when reading and how a reader's expression changes with the moods of the characters.

Parent Involvement

Standard: 5.10

Getting parents involved is an effective way to give your students a double dose of reading fluency practice. See the "Parent Letter" activity on page 74.

High-Frequency Words

Standard: 5.8

Knowledge of high-frequency words provides students with the ability to read more smoothly as they encounter fewer unfamiliar words.

Materials
- copies of high-frequency word cards (pages 66–71)
- scissors

1. Duplicate the word cards on pages 66–71 and cut them apart. (Laminate them for durability.)
2. Explain to the students that many words appear in print quite regularly. With these kinds of words, it is best to memorize them so they can be recognized automatically.
3. Mix up the cards and select a few words a day to review with the class. Be sure to review the pronunciation and use of each new word.
4. As new words are reviewed each day, add them to the stack and have the class work to recognize more and more new words.
5. For additional practice, place the cards at a learning center and encourage students to quiz each other in a word flash card game.
6. Assess students' knowledge of high-frequency words using the charts on pages 72–73.

High-Frequency Word Cards

about	after	again
always	and	because
been	before	both
came	carry	come

High-Frequency Word Cards *(cont.)*

could	does	done
down	eight	everything
find	found	four
friend	goes	going

High-Frequency Word Cards *(cont.)*

have	here	into
just	kind	know
laugh	light	little
live	look	made

High-Frequency Word Cards *(cont.)*

make	many	most
much	never	new
nothing	now	once
one	over	own

High-Frequency Word Cards *(cont.)*

please	put	question
read	right	said
saw	say	some
soon	thank	the

High-Frequency Word Cards *(cont.)*

their	them	there
us	use	very
want	wear	were
where	which	yours

High-Frequency Words Assessment

Student's Name: _____

Place a checkmark (✓) beside each word the student recognizes automatically.

Word	✓
about	
after	
again	
always	
and	
because	
been	
before	
both	
came	
carry	
come	
could	
does	
done	
down	
eight	
everything	

Word	✓
find	
found	
four	
friend	
goes	
going	
have	
here	
into	
just	
kind	
know	
laugh	
light	
little	
live	
look	
made	

High-Frequency Words Assessment *(cont.)*

Student's Name: _____

Place a checkmark (✓) beside each word the student recognizes automatically.

Word	✓
make	
many	
most	
much	
never	
new	
nothing	
now	
once	
one	
over	
own	
please	
put	
question	
read	
right	
said	

Word	✓
saw	
say	
some	
soon	
thank	
the	
their	
them	
there	
us	
use	
very	
want	
wear	
were	
where	
which	
yours	

More General Activities

Practice Makes Perfect

Standard: 5.9, 5.10

Most of us know the feeling of having to read "on the spot." How many of us remember counting ahead by sentences or paragraphs to look at the text we would be asked to read aloud? You can ease this anxiety in your students by allowing them to practice reading the passages silently before they are asked to read aloud. This allows each student the chance to familiarize himself or herself with the passage and focus on reading smoothly and with expression. You'll even notice that the students are more likely to listen to their peers read once the anxiety is relieved.

Parent Letter

Standard: 5.10

It is always a great idea to get parents involved with their children's reading development. While many parents are willing to do this, they are sometimes unaware of how to make home reading experiences successful. You can share with your students' parents how to make reading enjoyable by doing the following:

- reading aloud
- taking turns reading passages
- being an expressive reader
- allowing a child to practice before reading aloud

Duplicate the parent letter on page 75 and send it home to parents to provide them with more detailed ways to read to and with their children.

Be Our Guest

Standard: 5.10

Your students will enjoy hearing many different people read to them. You might want to make the role of Guest Reader one of your parent helper jobs. These experiences will demonstrate to your students that many people value and enjoy reading.

Materials
- copies of the "Be Our Guest" invitation on page 76

1. Ask interested parents to visit the classroom at a particular day and time.
2. You can provide the books for the parent or have him or her select a few favorites.
3. You might also want to invite other people to be guest readers, such as the principal, the P.E. teacher, the art teacher, a custodian, etc.
4. Use the letter on page 76 as an invitation for your guest readers.

Parent Letter

Dear Parent,

We are working on improving fluency when reading. You can assist your child with fluency in several ways:

1. Read aloud to your child. It's good for your child to read to you, but it is still very important for him or her to hear examples of good reading. So, head to the library, pick out a great book, and enjoy reading aloud to your child.

2. Be reading partners. Take turns reading with your child. You can take turns reading sentences and paragraphs, or you can read a sentence and have your child repeat the same sentence. This will assist your child with fluency as he or she copies your smooth reading.

3. Be expressive. Model for your child how to read with expression. Your child is learning to read basic text with expression, as well as using different expression when characters in the story have dialog. As your child improves expression, you'll notice reading that is smooth and pleasing to the ear.

4. Practice. Before having your child read aloud to you, allow him or her to practice the passage first. This will ensure that your child is familiar with the text and can focus on fluency and expression.

Your participation with fluency development is greatly appreciated. Happy reading!

Sincerely,

_____
(*teacher's signature*)

Be Our Guest

Dear _____,

The students in _____'s class would like to invite you to be a guest reader in our classroom. Would you like to join us? If so, would you like to:

❑ Bring your favorite children's book to class.

❑ Ask the teacher to select a book for you to read.

Please indicate below when you would like to visit our class.

_____

We look forward to your visit and listening to our new guest reader.

Sincerely,

_____

Reading Levels

When working on fluency development, it is important to select text that is at students' independent reading levels. You will need to designate different passages for students to ensure that they are working with text that is at the appropriate level. The National Reading Panel (2001) suggests the following for determining reading levels:

✏ **Independent Level**

This refers to easy text in which only 1 in 20 words are difficult for the student. The student should have a 95% success rate.

✏ **Instructional Level**

This text is more challenging, but not too difficult. The student should only encounter 1 in 10 difficult words with a 90% success rate.

✏ **Frustration Level**

This level refers to text that is very challenging for the child, with more than 1 in 10 difficult words. The student would have less than a 90% rate of success.

Rule of Thumb

Standard: 5.9

Teaching children to identify their own independent reading levels can be fairly difficult. While you can use the information about independent, instructional, and frustration levels to make determinations for your students, you can use the following strategy to help students select books on their own. Tell your students to follow this procedure:

1. A child selects a book and begins to read the first page.

2. When the child encounters a difficult word, he or she holds up a finger. The child continues in this manner while reading the page.

3. If the child finishes the passage without holding up all five fingers, the book is probably at an appropriate reading level.

4. However, if the child holds up all four fingers and then reaches the thumb, the book is probably too difficult.

More Fluency Activities

Do Not Disturb

Standard: 5.10

When learning to increase fluency, it is important for children to hear themselves reading. To allow your students the chance to practice, provide a quiet corner in your classroom for this purpose. Create a quiet corner by using bookcases, file cabinets, rolling chalk or white boards, etc., to form the walls of this area. Provide pillows or carpet squares to add comfort. Depending on the available light in this corner, you may want to provide a lamp. This will also create a peaceful environment in the corner. Review your expectations of the use of this area, including the number of students allowed, noise level, and purpose. You may want to post a rotating schedule to designate when students will have the opportunity to visit the quiet corner.

Who's on the Phone?

Standard: 5.9, 5.10

Having all students read aloud at once can create a rather chaotic classroom environment. Alleviate this problem by making individual "telephones" for your students.

Materials

- two PVC elbow joints (per child)
- 3"-long (7.5 cm) PVC pipe (per child)

1. To make a telephone, you need two PVC pipe elbow joints and a straight piece of PVC pipe measuring approximately three inches (7.5 cm).

2. Attach the elbows to each end of the straight pipe.

3. Turn both elbows in the same direction, so one opening can be held by the ear, while the other opening is situated near the mouth.

4. When the child speaks softly into the mouthpiece, his or her voice will be amplified in the earpiece.

5. Have students practice smooth reading as they speak into the PVC telephone.

More Fluency Activities *(cont.)*

Read Ahead

Standard: 5.9, 5.10

If you will be working with your students in small reading groups, allow the students to practice reading the text before group time.

1. Provide the passages that will be used and instruct the students to review the text during independent work time.

2. When students come to the reading group, they will be prepared to smoothly read the text with expression.

3. They will also be prepared to discuss the content of the text. Remember that when practicing fluency, the text should be at a reading level that is appropriate for each student.

Encountering New Words

Standard: 5.8

Encountering new words can create problems with fluent reading.

Materials

- index cards
- marker

1. To assist your children, provide index cards with new words printed on them. Review the words with the students. Be sure to review the words' meanings, as well as their pronunciations.

2. You might want to place groups of words in plastic sandwich bags in a learning center for the children to review.

3. When students are ready to read the story where the words appear, review the words once again. Then allow the students to practice reading the text silently before reading aloud.

4. Remember that the goal of fluency practice is to focus on smooth reading and expression, rather than on decoding text or deciphering meaning.

More Fluency Activities *(cont.)*

Read Me a Poem

Standard: 5.10

Listening to and reading poetry is a great way to assist children in developing fluency. Read many forms of poetry aloud to your students. Be sure to read poetry that is enjoyable to children. The poems of Shel Silverstein and Jack Prelutsky will keep your students laughing, while poems from the *Random House Book of Children's Poetry* will introduce your students to traditional rhymes. Draw attention to the cadence of your voice as you read. Assign short passages of poetry to pairs of students and have them practice reading with fluency.

Reading Big Books

Standard: 5.10

Big books can be very useful for teaching children about fluency. You can use these large-print stories to draw attention to groupings of words, pauses when reading, and expression.

1. Display a big book on an easel or the chalk tray on your chalkboard.

2. Point to each word as you read. Focus on the following skills:

   - Demonstrate the difference between choppy reading and smooth reading. Ask the students which form of reading is more pleasing to the ear.

   - Show the students how to pause when a comma is encountered.

   - Demonstrate the difference between reading in monotone and reading with expression. Draw attention to the tone of your voice as you read.

   - Demonstrate the way the voice can change when reading dialog to match the personality of a character.

Be sure to make the big book available to students during free time or at a learning center to allow them to practice these skills independently or with partners.

Student/Adult Reading Activity

Classroom Helpers

Standard: 5.10

While silent reading should be an integral part of every reading program, fluency practice requires reading aloud. Students are often more motivated to read aloud when someone is listening. This is a great job for classroom helpers.

Materials

- copies of the guide sheet below

1. Have a parent or classroom assistant work individually with students for short intervals. (Be sure the parent is comfortable working one on one with the students.) If desired, provide the list below to assist the helpers with this task.

2. Duplicate a copy of the chart on page 82 and a copy of the explanations on page 83.

3. Ask the classroom helper to record the name of each student with whom he or she worked and the child's progress during that session.

4. Be sure to have the helper ask and record the child's comments about the reading. This will provide important information about how the child views himself or herself as a reader. (You can also use the chart to record the progress you notice with each student.)

Guide to Fluency Practice

- ✏ Be sure the child has selected a book at his or reading level. There should be no more than 1 in 20 difficult words.

- ✏ Ask the child to read a passage to you. (Pay attention to the child's reading rate, fluency, and expression.)

- ✏ Assist the child in reading smoothly by modeling the reading of a sentence and then asking the child to repeat it.

- ✏ Try reading the passage together. Read at a comfortable rate and be sure to add expression.

- ✏ For more fluent readers, focus on the use of expression and a pleasing voice tone.

Fluency Progress

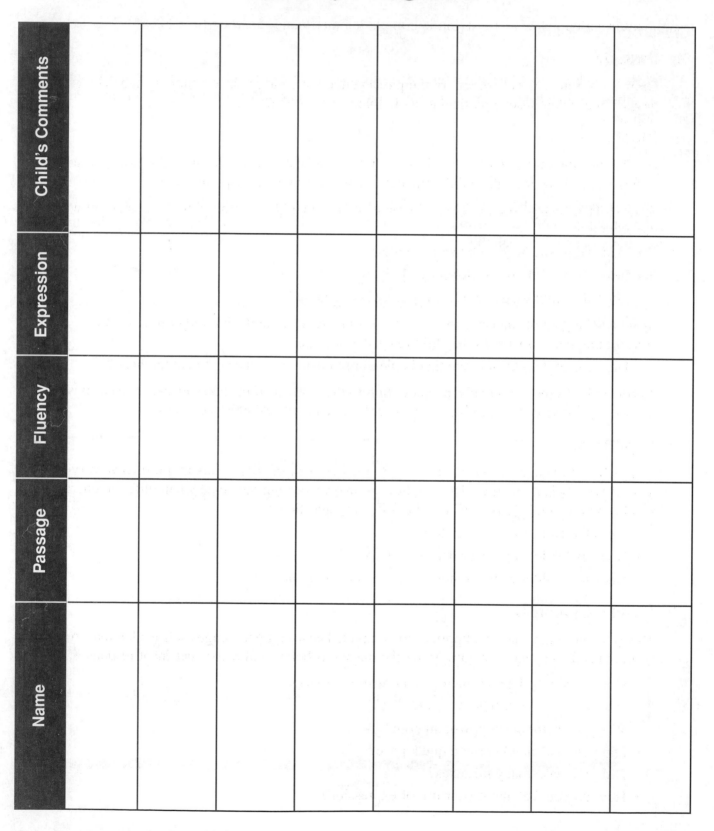

Name	Passage	Fluency	Expression	Child's Comments

Fluency Progress *(cont.)*

Use the information below to assist you in completing the fluency chart on page 82.

⁜ Passage

On this portion of the chart, record the passage that the child read. You might state that the passage was taken from a particular book, magazine, or text.

⁜ Fluency

For this portion of the chart, you will record the child's ability to read smoothly, quickly, and with accuracy. Comment on the child's fluency according to the descriptions below.

Smooth Reading—Listen as the child reads the passage. Pay attention to the manner in which the child reads.

- Does he or she hesitate between words?
- Does the reading sound "choppy"?
- Does the child have a consistent pace when reading?

Speed—The goal of fluency is not to read as quickly as possible, but rather to read at a comfortable pace. Listen as the child reads the passage.

- Does the child read at a rate that is pleasant to listen to and easy to comprehend?

Accuracy—As the child reads, pay attention to the number of mistakes made. The child would receive a positive comment if he or she is able to read with 80–90% accuracy.

⁜ Expression

Part of fluent reading involves the ability to read with expression. This might involve varying the tone of voice when reading. This might also involve varying the voice when different characters speak. As the child reads, consider the following questions:

- Does the child read in monotone?
- Does the child vary his or her tone of voice?
- Does the child vary his or her voice when reading dialog?

⁜ Child's Comments

This portion of the chart is important to complete because it encourages self-evaluation. After the child reads the passage, ask him or her the questions below and record pertinent responses.

- How do you feel about the way you read the passage?
- Was the passage difficult for you?
- Was your reading choppy or smooth?
- Did you read slowly or at a quick pace?
- Did you make many mistakes?
- How do you feel about your use of expression?

Choral-Reading Activities

Big Book Read-Alouds

Standard: 5.10

Big books are not only an excellent tool for modeling reading, they are also useful for choral reading. The large print in these books makes it possible for a group to see and read text at the same time.

Materials

- big book
- easel or chalkboard tray
- pointer (optional)

1. To engage your students in the choral reading of a big book, display the book on an easel or the chalk tray of the chalkboard.

2. Use a pointer or your finger to point to the words as the children read them aloud together.

3. Assist the children in establishing a rhythm to their group reading. Feel free to repeat the reading of particular pages.

4. Draw students' attention to places where pauses are appropriate and emphasize the use of expression.

5. Periodically, you may want to model the reading of a page and then ask the students to copy your rate and expression by choral reading again.

Totally Predictable

Standard: 5.10

The reading of predictable books is a great way to increase children's reading fluency. Children are able to focus on the quick and accurate reading of text rather than focusing on decoding. On page 85 you will find a list of predictable books that you can use with your students. Page 86 provides a parent letter explaining the benefits of reading predictable books.

Making Comparisons

Standard: 5.10

Help increase students' fluency by drawing their attention to voice, tone, and expression.

1. Demonstrate the importance of reading fluency by having your students read different kinds of books and poetry to compare reading tone, expression, etc. For example, the books *Silly Sally* and *King Bidgood's in the Bathtub* by Audrey Wood have fun, rhythmic tones. *Silly Sally* even utilizes a rhyming pattern.

2. On the other hand, *The Tenth Good Thing About Barney* by Judith Viorst is written in more of a conversational way and has a sullen tone related to the sad content of the story.

3. Read different forms of writing and draw students' attention to the tone, mood, and rhythm of your voice.

Predictable Books

Ahlberg, Janet. *Each Peach Pear Plum.* Penguin USA, 1999.

Barrett, Judi. *Animals Should Definitely Not Wear Clothing.* Aladdin Library, 1988.

Carle, Eric. *The Very Hungry Caterpillar.* Putnam Pub Group, 1983.

Christelow, Eileen. *Five Little Monkeys Jumping on the Bed.* Houghton Mifflin Co., 1998.

Gag, Wanda. *Millions of Cats.* Paper Star, 1996.

Geddes, Anne. *10 in the Bed.* Andrews McMeel Publishing, 2001.

Hoberman, Mary Ann. *A House Is a House for Me.* Viking Press, 1978.

Hutchins, Pat. *Rosie's Walk.* Scott Foresman, 1971.

Kalan, Robert. *Jump, Frog, Jump!* William Morrow, 1995.

Keats, Ezra. *Over in the Meadow.* Puffin, 1999.

Martin, Bill Jr. *Brown Bear, Brown Bear, What Do You See?* Henry Holt & Company, Inc., 1996.

Martin, Bill Jr. *Chicka Chicka Boom Boom.* Aladdin Library, 2000.

Munsch, Robert. *50 Below Zero.* Annick Press, 1992.

Numeroff, Laura Joffe. *If You Give a Mouse a Cookie.* Laura Geringer, 1985.

Raffi. *Wheels on the Bus (Raffi Songs to Read.)* Crown Books for Young Readers, 1998.

Rosen, Michael. *We're Going on a Bear Hunt.* Aladdin Library, 2003.

Shaw, Nancy. *Sheep in a Jeep.* Houghton Mifflin Co., 1997.

Stevens, Janet. *The House That Jack Built.* Holiday House, 1985.

Viorst, Judith. *Alexander and the Terrible, Horrible, No Good, Very Bad Day.* Aladdin Library, 1987.

Wood, Audrey. *King Bidgood's in the Bathtub.* Harcourt, 1985.

Wood, Audrey. *The Napping House.* Red Wagon Books, 2000.

Wood, Audrey. *Silly Sally.* Red Wagon Books, 1999.

Predictable Books *(cont.)*

Dear Parent,

As you know, we are working on reading fluency in class. You can assist your child in reading quickly and accurately by reading predictable books. A list of predictable books is provided below. I encourage you to check out some of these books from the library and read them to and with your child.

Reading fluency can be improved through the use of choral reading. Choral reading is when two or more people read the same text at the same time. You can read a predictable book with your child or even invite other adults or siblings to read with you. You'll find this to be a fun and engaging experience for all of you.

Happy reading!

Sincerely,

_____
(*teacher's signature*)

Predictable Books

- ✏ *Alexander and the Terrible, Horrible, No Good, Very Bad Day* by Judith Viorst
- ✏ *Animals Should Definitely Not Wear Clothing* by Judi Barrett
- ✏ *Five Little Monkeys Jumping on the Bed* by Eileen Christelow
- ✏ *A House is a House for Me* by Mary Ann Hoberman
- ✏ *If You Give a Mouse a Cookie* by Laura Joffe Numeroff
- ✏ *King Bidgood's in the Bathtub* by Audrey Wood
- ✏ *Millions of Cats* by Wanda Gag
- ✏ *The Napping House* by Audrey Wood
- ✏ *Over in the Meadow* by Ezra Jack Keats
- ✏ *Sheep in a Jeep* by Nancy Shaw
- ✏ *Wheels on the Bus: Raffi Songs to Read* by Raffi

Tape-Assisted Reading Activities

These activities provide students with reading models to help them develop their own fluency.

Audio Books

Standard: 5.10

Materials

- audio recording of a children's book
- printed form of the book
- tape recorder or CD player
- headphones

1. Set up a listening center with a tape recorder (or CD player) and headphones.
2. At the center, a child plays the recording and follows along in the book as the narrator reads.
3. Remind the child to pay attention to the smooth way in which the narrator reads and the expression in the narrator's voice.
4. Provide different kinds of audio books. The more examples of smooth, accurate reading a child experiences, the better he or she will learn to improve fluency.

Follow the Narrator

Standard: 5.10

Materials

- audio recording of a children's book
- printed form of the book
- tape recorder or CD player
- headphones

1. Similar to the activity above, set up a listening center with a tape recorder or CD player, headphones, and an audio recording of a book (including a printed copy of the book).
2. While the narrator reads, have the child follow along by pointing to the words as they are read.
3. After listening to the story once, instruct the child to listen again. This time the child reads along with the narrator, attempting to follow the narrator's reading rate, pauses, and expression.

Your Voice on Tape

Standard: 5.9, 5.10

Encourage your students to take responsibility for their fluency development with this activity.

Materials

- tape recorder with microphone
- children's book or passage of text

1. Provide a tape recorder and a microphone at a learning center (in a quiet area).
2. Instruct a student to select a passage of text and practice reading it several times.
3. Then the child records himself or herself reading the passage.
4. Finally, have the child listen to the tape recording. Ask the child to evaluate his or her reading and determine areas of improvement.
5. Duplicate copies of page 88 to guide the students as they evaluate their fluency.

Fluency Evaluation

Student Directions: Practice reading a passage of text. Record your voice as you read the passage. Listen to your recording. Complete the evaluation below.

Date of reading: _____

Passage read: _____

_____

Did I read smoothly? _____

Did I read quickly? _____

Did I make mistakes? _____

My plan for improvement: _____

_____

_____

_____

_____

Partner-Reading Activity

Student Pairs

Standard: 5.10

Paired student reading is another way that students can practice fluency. You will need to think about the combinations of students that you pair together. If you choose mixed-ability grouping, a struggling reader will be able to hear smooth and accurate reading from a fluent reader. By pairing students with equal abilities, students can set common goals and work together to read with fluency. Duplicate the form below for students. Have each student place the form in a reading folder. Each student should complete the form after a partner reading session.

Partner Reading Chart

Date: _____ My Partner: _____

Book Title: _____

Here's how it went: _____

_____

Date: _____ My Partner: _____

Book Title: _____

Here's how it went: _____

_____

Date: _____ My Partner: _____

Book Title: _____

Here's how it went: _____

_____

Date: _____ My Partner: _____

Book Title: _____

Here's how it went: _____

_____

Readers-Theater Activities

What Is It?

Standard: 5.9, 5.10

Readers Theater is a fun way for children to practice oral reading with fluency. There are many ways it can be implemented in the classroom.

✢ Teacher/Group Reading

For this kind of Readers Theater, the teacher has the primary reading role. The script contains repetitive parts that the children join in on.

✢ Quick Scripts

With quick scripts, the children practice short readings on different occasions. The scripts are reintroduced periodically for fluency practice.

✢ Rehearsed Reading for Performance

These can involve short or long scripts that the children practice for the purpose of performing for the class.

To begin, children need to understand the purpose of Readers Theater. Gather them together in a group and read a short passage from a familiar story, such as "The Three Little Pigs." Discuss the events of the story. Ask them how the pigs might have felt.

- How would they speak to the wolf?
- Were they frightened?
- Were they angry?
- How would their voices sound when they spoke?
- How would the wolf's voice sound when he spoke to the pigs?

Invite students to recite dialog from "The Three Little Pigs" using appropriate expressions. Explain that when performing Readers Theater, it is important to assume the role of the character and speak in the same way that the character would speak.

Pages 91–93 provide ideas for Readers Theater scripts and a script-planning sheet for Readers Theater.

Important Tips

- Always allow children to review and practice scripts before reading aloud.
- Encourage children to use expression when they read.
- Encourage the children to read as smoothly as possible.
- Allow time for the children to rehearse their lines before a performance.

Readers-Theater Activities *(cont.)*

Create a Play

Standards: 5.9, 5.10

Show students how to create a Readers Theater script using a passage of text that contains dialog.

Materials

- passage of text (with dialog)
- chart paper
- marker
- copies of planning sheet (page 93)

1. Draw students' attention to the characters included in the dialog and have them determine whether or not the passage would require a narrator.

2. Write the script on chart paper, writing a character's name and the dialog he or she says.

3. Explain that for a Readers Theater performance, a person needs to be selected for each character and the narrator.

4. After demonstrating how to create a script from text, have students create their own scripts.

5. Duplicate page 93 and have students use the planning sheet as a guide.

Story Summaries

Standards: 5.9, 5.10, and 7.3

Another way to have students create their own Readers Theater scripts is to have them summarize stories and create their own dialog.

Materials

- copies of planning sheet (page 93)

1. Rather than taking dialog straight from the story, students recall the most important events and dialog exchanges and then write a script that summarizes the story.

2. Have the students write the script in the same manner described above with each character's name and dialog beside it.

3. The students can use the same planning sheet on page 93.

Stories for Readers Theater

Many stories lend themselves to the Readers Theater format. The following is a list of stories from which to choose and the characters they feature:

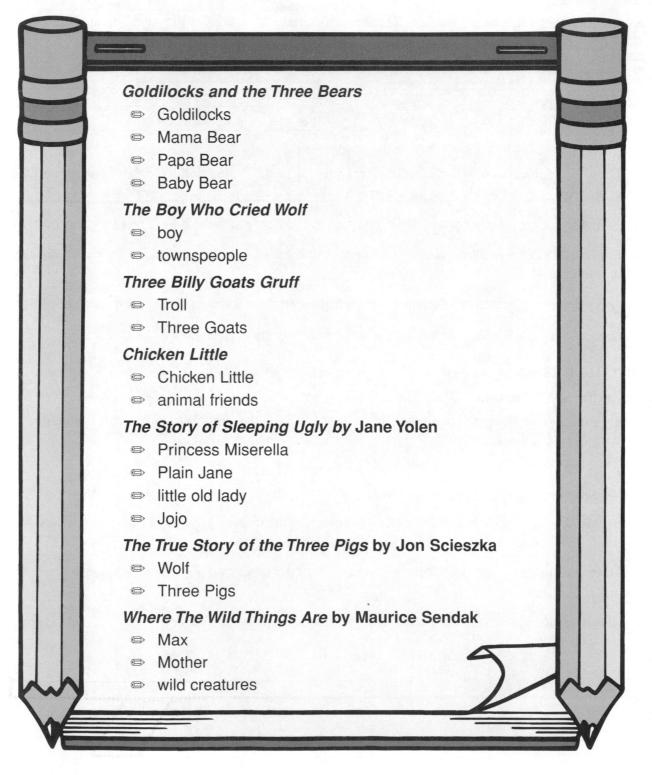

Goldilocks and the Three Bears
- Goldilocks
- Mama Bear
- Papa Bear
- Baby Bear

The Boy Who Cried Wolf
- boy
- townspeople

Three Billy Goats Gruff
- Troll
- Three Goats

Chicken Little
- Chicken Little
- animal friends

The Story of Sleeping Ugly by Jane Yolen
- Princess Miserella
- Plain Jane
- little old lady
- Jojo

The True Story of the Three Pigs by Jon Scieszka
- Wolf
- Three Pigs

Where The Wild Things Are by Maurice Sendak
- Max
- Mother
- wild creatures

Planning Sheet

Passage Used: _____

_____

Narrator: _____

Rehearsal Time: _____

Write the script in the frame below.

Character Names	Actor/Actress

Reading Inventories

There are a variety of books of reading inventories that can be used to assess your students' reading progress. Information from these inventories can assist you in understanding reading difficulties and progress, as well as providing useful information for parents.

- *Qualitative Reading Inventory-3* (3rd Edition) by Lauren Leslie and Joanne Caldwell. Pearson Allyn & Bacon, 2000.

- *Informal Reading Inventory: Preprimer to Twelfth Grade* by Paul C. Burns and Betty D. Roe. Houghton Mifflin, 2002.

- *Bader Reading and Language Inventory and Readers Passages Pkg.* (4th Edition) by Lois A. Bader. Prentice Hall, 2001.

- *Classroom Reading Inventory* (9th Edition) by Nicholas J. Silvaroli, et al. McGraw-Hill, 2000.

- *Reading Miscue Inventory: Alternative Procedures* by Yetta M. Goodman, et al. Richard C. Owen Publishing, 1987.

- *Qualitative Reading Inventory* by Lauren Leslie, Joanne Caldwell. HarperCollins College Division, 1994.

- *Basic Reading Inventory (including CD-ROM)* by Jerry Johns. Kendall/Hunt Publishing Company; 8th Edition (May 25, 2001).

- *Diagnostic Reading Inventory for Primary & Intermediate Grades* by Janet M. Scott and Sheila C. McCleary. Scott & McCleary; 3rd Edition (2003).

- *Informal Reading-Thinking Inventory* by Anthony V. Manzo, et al. Wadsworth Publishing; 1st Edition (January 1, 1995).

Reading-Level Calculation

According to *Put Reading First* (2001, page 29), you can calculate the correct words per minute with the following formula:

1. Select two passages of text at the child's grade level (not reading level).
2. Have a student read each passage aloud for exactly one minute.
3. Count the number of words the child read in both passages. Divide by two to get the *average number of words read per minute.*
4. Determine the number of words read incorrectly in both passages. Divide by two to get the *average number of errors per minute.*
5. Subtract the *average number of errors per minute* from the *average number of words read per minute* to get the **words correct per minute** (WPCM).
6. Repeat this process a few times during the school year to assess each student's progress. See page 96 for a chart to record student progress.

> This chart can be used as a guideline for average fluency goals:
>
>   ✏ 60 WCPM = end of first grade
>
>   ✏ 90–100 WCPM = end of second grade
>
>   ✏ 114 WCPM = end of third grade

Word-Processing Reading Level Tool

Some word-processing programs have tools you can use to determine the reading level of a passage.

Materials

- word-processing program with a reading-level tool
- passage of text

1. Open *Microsoft Word* and paste your reading passage into a new document.
2. Click on the **Tools** menu at the top of the screen and select **Preferences** or **Options**.
3. Click on the **Spelling and Grammar** tab from the resulting window.
4. Then click to make a check mark beside **Show Readability Statistics,** and click OK.
5. Highlight a passage of text and then click on the **Tools Menu**.
6. Select **Spelling and Grammar**.
7. After the program runs a spell check, a window will appear.
8. At the bottom of this window, you will see **Flesch-Kincaid Grade Level**. The grade level of the passage will be listed beside it. (If you have a word-processing program other than *Microsoft Word*, search the **Help** tool of your program for a readability tool. Follow the instructions for your word-processing program.)

Reading-Level Chart

Child's Name: _____

Date	Passage(s) Read	WCPM	Fluency	Comments

Fluency Progress Graph

Use the graph below to track a student's fluency progress. Calculate words correct per minute or WCPM (page 95) and plot fluency readings throughout the year. This will provide a visual record of progress to show to parents.

Name _____

Words Correct Per Minute									
150									
140									
130									
120									
110									
100									
90									
80									
70									
60									
50									
40									
30									
20									
Date									

Vocabulary

In order to communicate effectively, we need to have an adequate vocabulary. This is typically discussed in terms of oral vocabulary and reading vocabulary, but also includes listening and writing vocabulary. **Reading vocabulary** is the words we recognize and understand when we read; **oral vocabulary** is the words we use when speaking; **listening vocabulary** is the words we understand when listening to others speak; and **writing vocabulary** is the words we use in our own writing.

Vocabulary is important because children use their vocabulary to make sense of print. It can be taught **directly** or **indirectly**.

☞ **Indirect Vocabulary Learning**

Most vocabulary is learned indirectly. It happens as we communicate through speaking and writing in everyday life. When we hear or see words used in different concepts, it helps us to expand our knowledge of word meanings. This book provides indirect vocabulary activities in the following areas:

- daily oral language
- adult read-alouds
- independent reading

☞ **Direct Vocabulary Learning**

Some vocabulary is learned directly. This involves explicit instruction of individual words. While most vocabulary is learned indirectly, direct vocabulary instruction can be helpful to children for reading comprehension. Direct vocabulary learning involves **specific-word instruction** and **word learning strategies**.

With specific word instruction, students are taught individual words and their meanings. This is typically done to prepare students for text they will be reading. Specific-word instruction increases students' reading comprehension, is particularly effective when children are actively involved, and helps children remember word meanings when they are used in different contexts.

Because it isn't possible to teach children the meanings and pronunciations of all words they will encounter, it is important to teach children strategies to use when they encounter new words. This book provides such word learning strategies as dictionary skills, knowledge of word parts, and using context clues.

Cautions about Vocabulary Instruction

- ✏ Children can be overwhelmed if too many words are introduced at one time. Focus only on a few words at a time

- ✏ Don't spend too much time on meanings of words in isolation. This could interfere with comprehension of words in context.

- ✏ Don't spend too much time directly teaching words that can easily be understood in context.

- ✏ Remember that students need to learn what to do when they encounter new words. Be sure to spend more time teaching strategies rather than individual words.

- ✏ Remember that children internalize the meaning of a word when they have many opportunities to encounter it (especially in different contexts).

General Vocabulary Activities

Conversational Vocabulary

Standard: 7.4

In order for children to internalize new vocabulary words, they must hear them used often and in different ways. One way to remind students of the meanings of new words is to use them interchangeably with familiar words. For example, a teacher might say, "Be sure to write an adjective, a describing word that tells about the character." By pairing a new word with its synonym, your children will begin to recognize the use and meaning of the new word.

Interesting Words

Standard: 5.8

Encourage your students to begin a collection of new words.

Materials

- copy of page 104 for each student
- pencil

1. Duplicate a copy of page 104 for each student. You might want to have each student keep the page in a special folder.
2. The student records a new word in the first column.
3. In the second column, the student writes where he or she found the word (a book, through conversation, etc.).
4. Next, the student writes the definition of the word.
5. In the last column, the student writes how the word was originally used.
6. Provide extra sheets of page 104 so students can continue collecting words throughout the year.

Synonyms and Antonyms

Standard: 5.8

This activity allows your students to practice identifying pairs of words that have same or opposite meanings.

Materials

- cards on pages 100–103
- marker

1. Duplicate the cards on pages 100–103.
2. Display two words (from the same pair) at a time.
3. Ask the students to read the words and determine whether the words have similar meanings or opposite meanings.
4. Explain that words that mean the same are called *synonyms* and that words that have opposite meanings are called *antonyms*.
5. Continue in this manner with different sets of words.
6. To make this activity a learning center, mark the backs of the cards with colored dots or another kind of symbol for self-checking.

Synonym Cards

fix	**repair**
hug	**embrace**
smile	**grin**
eat	**gobble**
chair	**seat**
friend	**buddy**

Synonym Cards *(cont.)*

laugh	**giggle**
car	**auto**
soggy	**wet**
watch	**look**
street	**road**
close	**shut**

Antonym Cards

fast	**slow**
laugh	**cry**
destroy	**create**
high	**low**
asleep	**awake**
sick	**well**

Antonym Cards *(cont.)*

big	little
wide	thin
exciting	boring
run	walk
far	near
dark	light

Interesting Words

New Word	Where I Found It	Definition	How It Was Used

More General Activities

Definition Word Wall

Standard: 5.8

Teachers often use word walls to assist children with their spelling. Try a new twist on your classroom word wall with this activity.

Materials

- construction paper
- marker
- stapler or pushpins

1. Post new vocabulary words on a bulletin board or wall.

2. Below each word, write the definition and use the word in a sentence.

3. Review the word wall often and encourage the students to use these new words in their conversation and in writing.

4. Periodically invite students to contribute their own new words, definitions, and sentences to the wall.

Introducing Words

Standard: 5.8, 7.4

It is important to recognize that increased vocabulary leads to increased comprehension. Because of this, children benefit from the introduction of new words before reading a story for the first time.

Materials

- chart paper
- marker

1. Review a selected story and select 8 to 10 words that might be difficult for the students to read.

2. Write the words on cards or on chart paper.

3. Ask the students if they have heard or read any of the words before and if they know how the words can be used in sentences. Make sure the students can pronounce the words.

4. It may be necessary to show how a word is used in an actual sentence from the story. You will find that this form of vocabulary review helps children when they are reading, as they will read with better fluency and comprehension.

More General Vocabulary Activities *(cont.)*

Concept Development

Standard: 5.8

Introduction of new words is important when studying concept themes. For example, when studying about butterflies, children can learn words such as *pupa*, *larvae*, *lifecycle*, *metamorphosis*, etc. Begin by asking students to list words they know relating to the theme. Then introduce the new vocabulary words in the manner described on page 105 or allow students to determine the words' meanings in context. Be sure to provide opportunities for the students to encounter the words many times and in different contexts, so they will be able to develop a deeper understanding of them. Appropriate concept themes and vocabulary for second grade are listed in this chart:

Theme	Vocabulary
Weather	tornado, thunder, lightning, blizzard, temperature, thermometer, forecast
Insects	thorax, abdomen, lifecycle, pupa, larva, colony, pest
Matter	solid, liquid, gas, evaporation, solution, attribute, texture
Magnets	poles, attraction, repel, force
Health	nutrition, vitamins, minerals, balance, exercise

Great Read-Alouds

Standard: 5.8

The books below are great read-alouds for second grade. Below each title is a list of vocabulary words featured in the story that can be used for discussion. The chapter where each word can be found is listed in parentheses.

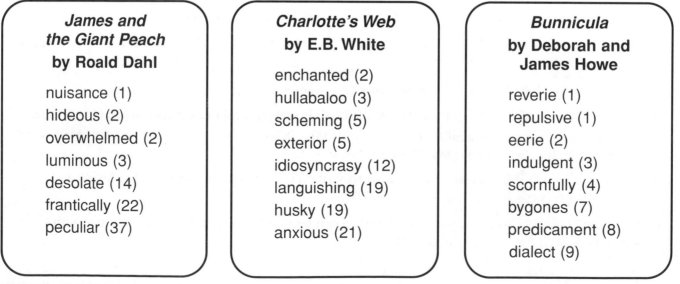

**James and
the Giant Peach
by Roald Dahl**

nuisance (1)
hideous (2)
overwhelmed (2)
luminous (3)
desolate (14)
frantically (22)
peculiar (37)

**Charlotte's Web
by E.B. White**

enchanted (2)
hullabaloo (3)
scheming (5)
exterior (5)
idiosyncrasy (12)
languishing (19)
husky (19)
anxious (21)

**Bunnicula
by Deborah and
James Howe**

reverie (1)
repulsive (1)
eerie (2)
indulgent (3)
scornfully (4)
bygones (7)
predicament (8)
dialect (9)

More General Vocabulary Activities *(cont.)*

Definition Boxes

Standard: 5.8

This activity is a great way to encourage your students to practice defining new vocabulary words.

Materials

- two small boxes (such as shoeboxes)
- marker
- index cards

1. Label the lids of the shoeboxes: **Words** and **Definitions**.

2. When reading a book or learning about a new theme, write new words on index cards. (Invite the students to suggest interesting new words.)

3. Ask the students to assist you with defining each new word.

4. Write each definition on an index card.

5. Put the index cards in the appropriate boxes and place them at a learning center.

6. To play, a child takes a word from the Words box and then looks for its definition in the Definitions box. When a match is found, the child places the cards side by side.

7. The goal is to match all words with their correct definitions.

Vocabulary Clues

Standard: 5.8

This interactive game provides your students with vocabulary fun!

Materials

- list of vocabulary words
- chair
- chalkboard
- chalk

1. Prepare for this activity by creating a list of relevant vocabulary words.

2. Divide the students into two teams. Place a chair in front of the chalkboard. The chair should be facing away from the chalkboard.

3. Team one selects a student to sit in the chair.

4. Write a vocabulary word from the list on the chalkboard (behind the student in the chair). The members of Team 1 then offer clues about the word. Students can act out the word or give verbal clues, such as synonyms and antonyms or definitions.

5. The goal is to get the student to say the word written on the chalkboard within a designated period of time (15–30 seconds, for example).

6. If the team is successful, it receives a point. Then team two plays in the same manner with a new word written on the chalkboard.

Wordplay Activities

Your children will get a kick out of these wordplay activities.

Idioms
Standard: 5.8

Vocabulary not only refers to the meanings of words, but also the way in which words are used. Learning about idioms is an entertaining way to improve children's knowledge of language. The following are common idioms that you can discuss with your students:

- frog in the throat
- fork in the road
- got up on the wrong side of the bed
- raining cats and dogs

Discuss the literal and figurative meanings of the idioms. Then have each student select an idiom and have him or her illustrate both the literal and figurative meanings. As an added activity, use pages 109–112 to create a learning center. Duplicate and cut apart the cards. The student then determines whether each picture is depicting the literal or figurative meaning of the idiom.

Puns
Standard: 5.8

A pun is a play on words, such as "Jamaican me crazy" or "Orange you glad I came over?" Encourage your students to create and share puns of their own. The books listed below can be used to provide the enjoyment of puns and assist the children in making their own.

1. Write the word *orange* on the chalkboard.
2. Explain that a pun is made when a word is used in a humorous way, such as:
   "Orange you glad I'm your friend?"
3. Draw attention to the fact that the word *orange* is used in place of the words *aren't you*.
4. Write the word *pun*. Point out that it rhymes with *fun* and could be used in place of that word, such as "Isn't this punny?"
5. Continue in this manner, allowing the children to create some of their own.
6. For additional practice with puns, have the children play the game on pages 113–115.

Books about Puns

Continue the fun of learning about puns by sharing these books:
- *It Looks a Lot Like Reindeer* by Brian P. Cleary
- *Jamaica Sandwich?* by Brian P. Cleary
- *Max's Wacky Taxi Day* by Max Grover
- *Pun and Games: Jokes, Riddles, Rhymes, Daffynitions, Tairy Fales, and More Wordplay for Kids* by Richard Lederer
- *The Weighty Word Book* by Paul M. Levitt, Douglas A. Gurger, Elissa S. Guralnick, and Janet Stevens
- *You Never Sausage Love* by Brian P. Cleary

Idiom Cards

beat around the bush

beat around the bush

Cut it out!

Cut it out!

hit the hay

hit the hay

Idiom Cards *(cont.)*

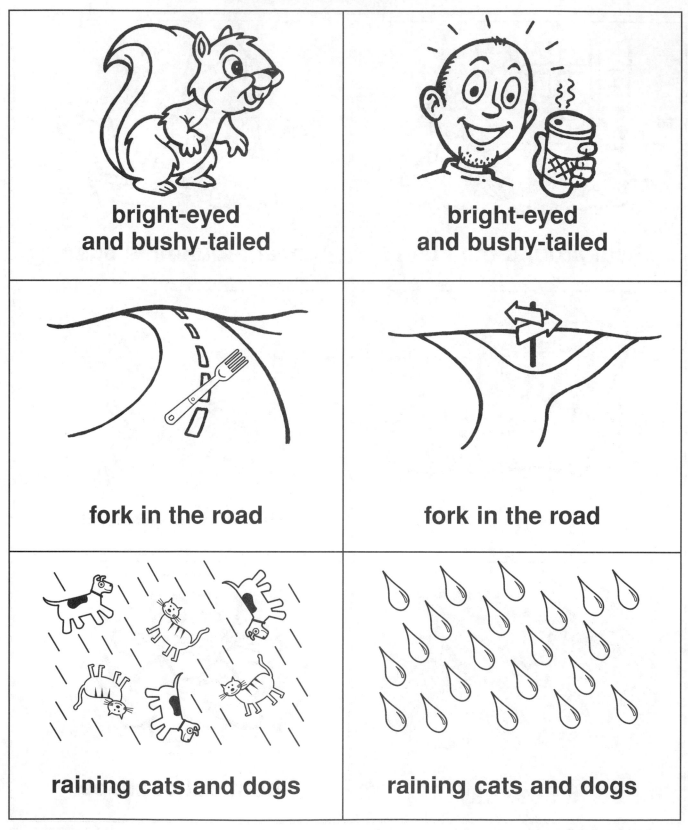

bright-eyed
and bushy-tailed

bright-eyed
and bushy-tailed

fork in the road

fork in the road

raining cats and dogs

raining cats and dogs

Idiom Cards *(cont.)*

got my eye on you	got my eye on you
under the weather	under the weather
bent out of shape	bent out of shape

Idiom Cards *(cont.)*

Pun and Games

Use these cards and the board on pages 114 and 115 to play a pun game. See the instructions on page 114.

Orange you glad we're friends?	Did you see the ghost and his ghoul friend?	The man yelled, "Please help! It's a matter of wife or death."
The funny story began, "Once a pun a time . . "	The tomato ran into the wall and said, "I was trying to ketchup!"	The mummy was just dying to go to the party.
This is all pun and games.	The duck got in trouble for using fowl language.	After she ate the seafood, she just clammed up.
The dirty truck auto be washed.	The clown is very punny.	The pony on the Ferris wheel was horsing around.

Now add some of your own.

Pun and Games *(cont.)*

Directions (for two players)

1. Player 1 places a game marker on **START**.

2. The player selects a card (see page 113) and reads the pun.

3. Player 1 determines the word that is used in a funny way.

4. If the player correctly identifies the word, he or she flips a coin. **Heads** = move ahead one space, **Tails** = move ahead two spaces.

5. Next, Player 2 takes a turn.

6. The first player to reach **FINISH** wins.

START

Pun and Games *(cont.)*

Read-Aloud Activities

New Words in Print

Standard: 5.4, 5.8

Reading aloud to children has many benefits that relate to all areas of reading development. The reading of stories can also help children to develop increased vocabulary. This can be done quite naturally in a daily read-aloud time in class. When new words are encountered, adults can pause to discuss them by asking the following questions:

- "Have you heard this word before?"
- "What do you think it means?"
- "Do you know of other words that sound the same or have similar parts?"
- "Listen to the way the word is used in a sentence. Does this give you clues to the word's meaning?"

While the discussion of new words during story time is important, it is also important to maintain the enjoyment of the story. Discuss new words—but don't discuss so many that the students lose track of the storyline.

Word Substitution

Standard: 5.4, 5.8, 7.4

After reading a short story, take time to identify new words. Once new words have been defined and discussed, have the students replace the new words with more familiar words.

Materials

- passage of text
- chart paper
- marker

1. After reading a new text aloud, write a passage on chart paper. Leave a blank line where a new word would be located. Ask students to think of synonyms for the missing word and write a familiar word in its place.

2. Have the students read the passage with the familiar word(s) in place. Discuss the fact that the use of new words can add interest to a story.

3. Try this activity in reverse by replacing common words with more interesting words.

4. Be sure to write and display the new passage and allow the children to read it aloud.

Independent Reading

Assist your students in determining the meanings of new words as they read silently. Duplicate a copy of the form below. In the first column, write words they will encounter in a story. You might also provide a blank copy for each student and have each child write new words found when reading. To complete the form, the student guesses the meanings of the new words based on how they are used in context. Be sure to review the new words with the students and discuss their processes for determining the definitions. Then provide actual meaning of each word for students to write in the third column.

Word	My Guess	Actual Meaning

Specific-Word-Instruction Activities

Word Illustrations

Standard: 5.8

One way to assist children in learning new words is to have them discuss and illustrate their meanings.

Materials

- white construction paper
- crayons
- marker
- children's book
- index cards

1. Provide each child with a large sheet of white construction paper.
2. Have the child fold the paper to make eight sections.
3. Select eight new words from a story.
4. Discuss one word at a time. Write the word on an index card and show the students the word. Ask them to try to pronounce it. Then model the correct pronunciation.
5. Ask if they know the meaning of the word. If they don't, discuss the word's meaning and use it in a sentence.
6. Each student should write the new word near the bottom of one of the construction-paper sections.
7. Above the word, the child should draw a picture that represents the word. You might also ask the child to write a sentence using the word.
8. Continue in this manner with the remaining words.
9. Remind the children that these words will be found in the story they will read. Encourage them to refer to their illustrations for assistance in remembering the meanings of the words.

The Sky's the Limit

Standard: 5.8

This activity assists your students in generating vocabulary words about clouds.

Materials

- *It Looked Like Spilt Milk* by Charles G. Shaw (*optional*)
- paper and pencils

1. Gather the students together and engage them in a discussion about clouds. Ask them if they have ever looked at the shapes of clouds and the kinds of shapes they have seen. If desired, share the book *It Looked Like Spilt Milk* by Charles G. Shaw.
2. Take the class outside on a cloudy day and have the students look up at the clouds. (You might want to find a grassy area where the children can lay down to look at the clouds.)
3. Ask the children to think of words that describe the clouds they see.
4. Upon returning to the classroom, have the students write down the words they thought of and discuss these words as a class. Wite student's words on chart paper.
5. Draw attention to the words that provide general descriptions (e.g., *pretty*, *cool*), as opposed to words that offer specific descriptions (e.g., *fluffy*, *misty*).

Specific-Word-Instruction Activities *(cont.)*

Adding Prefixes and Suffixes

Standard: 5.6, 5.8

Challenge your students to think of new words using prefixes and suffixes.

Materials

- chart paper
- marker
- writing paper
- pencils

1. In a group, discuss prefixes and suffixes with your students.

2. Explain that a *prefix* is a word part at the beginning of a word. For example, the prefix *un* can be added to the word *tie* to make the word *untie*.

3. Explain that a *suffix* is a word part at the end of a word. For example, the suffix *able* can be added to *comfort* to make the word *comfortable*.

4. Ask the students to think of other prefixes and suffixes they know. List these in two separate columns on chart paper. (See below.)

5. Post the lists in a prominent location in the classroom.

6. Distribute paper and pencils to students and instruct them to write down as many words as possible using the prefixes and suffixes listed.

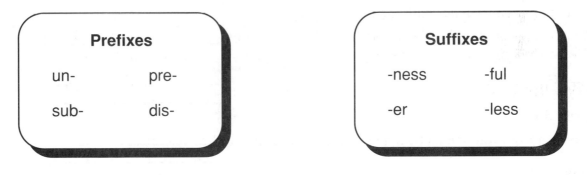

Prefixes	
un-	pre-
sub-	dis-

Suffixes	
-ness	-ful
-er	-less

Slang

Standard: 5.8

Your students will have fun discussing common slang words.

Materials

- copy of page 120
- pencils

1. Understanding the use of slang is important for a few reasons. First, children need to recognize slang spellings versus proper spellings of words. Second, children need to learn when slang is and is not appropriate.

2. Discuss slang words, such as *gotcha*, *lemme*, and *ain't*. Continue to practice by having each child complete page 120.

Is It or Isn't It?

Directions: Read each sentence below and determine whether or not slang is used. If the sentence uses a slang word, write **Slang**. Write **No Slang** if the sentence uses proper English.

1. Who's at the door? _

2. Look at what I gotcha. _ _ _ _ _ _ _ _ _ _ _ _ _ _ _ _

3. Lemme see the picture. _ _ _ _ _ _ _ _ _ _ _ _ _ _ _

4. That is a pretty dress you're wearing. _ _ _ _ _ _ _ _

5. Hey, Billy, wassup? _ _ _ _ _ _ _ _ _ _ _ _ _ _ _ _ _

6. I'm gonna go to Amy's house after school. _ _ _ _ _

7. I gotta go now. _

8. Terry is my best friend. _ _ _ _ _ _ _ _ _ _ _ _ _ _ _

9. Don't get upset. Just chill out! _ _ _ _ _ _ _ _ _ _

10. After my birthday party, I was, like, so happy. _ _ _

11. Will you meet me on the playground? _ _ _ _ _ _ _ _

12. I worked very hard on my homework. _ _ _ _ _ _ _ _

Extension: On the back of this page, rewrite the slang sentences using proper English.

Specific-Word-Instruction Activities *(cont.)*

Using New Words

Standard: 5.4, 5.8

Encourage your students to be aware of new words they hear in conversation and read in text. Make a list on chart paper of the new words they find and display it in the classroom. Discuss the words and their use and encourage the students to use the words in conversation and in writing. You should model the use of these words as well. Each student will be proud as they hear you and others using the words they added to the list.

Daily Word

Standard: 5.8

Collect new words encountered in text and use them as a part of a daily class activity. Write each new word on an index card. Upon entering the classroom in the morning, give each child a card. The child thinks about the meaning of the word and how it might be used in conversation. (Encourage the students to collaborate to determine the words' meanings.) The goal for each child is to use the word in conversation at least one time during the day. Distribute different words to different students each day. Periodically, change the group of words on index cards in order to provide the students with the opportunity to encounter new words throughout the year.

Using Children's Literature

Standard: 5.8

You can provide a variety of vocabulary activities that correspond with specific children's literature books. Three modern children's literature classics are listed below with the words that would need vocabulary instruction.

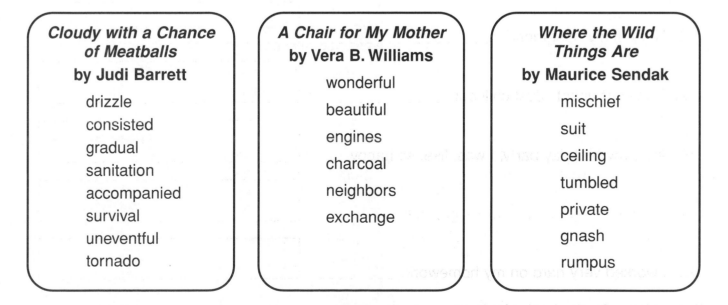

Cloudy with a Chance of Meatballs **by Judi Barrett**	*A Chair for My Mother* **by Vera B. Williams**	*Where the Wild Things Are* **by Maurice Sendak**
drizzle	wonderful	mischief
consisted	beautiful	suit
gradual	engines	ceiling
sanitation	charcoal	tumbled
accompanied	neighbors	private
survival	exchange	gnash
uneventful		rumpus
tornado		

Word-Learning Strategies

Finding Words

Standard: 5.8

Provide a copy of a selected children's book for each student. Ask students to look through the book in search of familiar words. Ask them to make a list of words as they find them. Work together to define the new words and then re-read the book. Have students discuss how their understanding of the book changed from the first reading to the second.

Using Context to Define Words

Standard: 5.4

This activity will help your students to determine word meanings.

1. Show the children how to use context to determine a word's meaning. For example, the book *Cloudy with a Chance of Meatballs* by Judi Barrett features the word *sanitation*.

2. Have the students read the word in the sentence where it is used in the story. Ask them if the sentence provides any clue as to the word's meaning. They will likely say it does not.

3. Direct the students to continue reading the sentences that follow. At this point, your students should be able to determine the fact that workers at a sanitation department clean things up.

4. Lead them to understand that the word *sanitation* refers to being clean.

Defining Words

Standard: 5.8

Work with the children to define the new words they find. This time have the students find definitions using different tools, such as dictionaries or a thesaurus in a word-processing program.

1. When using an electronic thesaurus, a student types a word into a word-processing document.

2. Then the student highlights the word by dragging the cursor over it.

3. Next, the student clicks on the **Tools** menu at the top of the screen and selects **Thesaurus**. (Depending on your operating system, you may have to locate the thesaurus in a different way, such as **Tools**, **Language**, and **Thesaurus**. Make adaptations as needed.) A dialog window will appear with a list of synonyms.

4. By reading through the list of synonyms, it is possible for the child to determine the word's meaning. See this example for the word *gradual:*

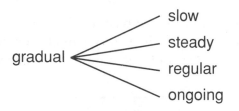

Word-Learning Strategies *(cont.)*

Practice, Practice

Standard: 5.4

Have the students practice identifying word meanings in context. Select a sentence that contains a vocabulary word of your choice. Display the sentence with the word underlined. Then provide several definition choices (one correct and the rest incorrect). Have the students determine the correct meaning of the underlined word by the way it is used in the sentence.

Play Cards

Standard: 5.8

Before having your students read a selected book, review some of the difficult words they will encounter. Write each word on an index card. Review the words one by one, asking the children to pronounce each one and try to use it in a sentence. In the book *A Chair for My Mother* by Vera B. Williams, you might select the following words:

- exchange
- neighbors
- charcoal
- engine
- beautiful
- wonderful

I'm Thinking Of . . .

Standard: 5.8

Allow the students to read a book at least one time. Then play a word-search game. For each vocabulary word, state a clue about it, such as "I'm thinking of a word that means the same as *great* or *amazing*." Have the children look for the word and answer the riddle.

Pre-Reading

Standard: 5.8

Some of the words in a particular story might be quite difficult for your students. Review these words ahead of time. Write the sentences from the book on the chalkboard or chart paper. Invite students to read the sentences and try to guess the meanings of the underlined vocabulary words. Write the meanings beside each sentence. Explain that these words will be found in the story. Encourage the students to refer to the group's definitions if they have trouble when reading the story.

Other Uses

Standard: 5.4

Understanding new words can be easier when they are used in different sentences. Explain to the students that the same vocabulary words used in a story can also be used in more common ways. List selected words on chart paper and ask the students to think of sentences using these words. Write their responses on the chart paper.

Word-Learning Strategies *(cont.)*

Word Forms

Standard: 5.8, 7.4

Many words that children encounter in reading have different forms. For example, the word *speak* has different forms, such as *speaker*, *speaks*, *speaking*, and *spoken*. These words probably don't need much explanation, but think about the word *vision*. If a student knows that vision is something that allows one to see, he or she might have an easier time understanding the words *visual* or *visualization*. Knowing the forms of a word can assist when new words are found. You should select words that your students will find in the stories they read. Take time to discuss these words as they are relevant to stories the students read. See the list below for other words with different forms.

- migrate, migration, migrant, immigration, migrating
- literature, literate, literacy
- grow, grew, growth
- capture, captive, captivate

Concept Vocabulary

Standard: 5.4

When studying a particular theme, such as "food and nutrition" or "the rainforest," have the students create their own vocabulary list to study.

Materials

- pieces of fruits and vegetables
- cubes of cheese
- nuts (*be sure to check for allergies*)
- beef jerky
- crackers
- paper plates
- chart paper
- marker

1. When participating in a unit about food and nutrition, bring in a variety of foods to sample, such as fruits, vegetables, cheese, etc.

2. Provide each student with a small plate of foods. As the students sample the foods, have them think about the appearances, flavors, and textures of the foods.

3. Invite them to share words that describe these characteristics as you write them on the chalkboard.

4. Review the vocabulary list periodically to remind the students of the words. (Use this same activity for other units. For the rainforest, have them create a word list after looking at pictures.)

Word of the Day

Standard: 5.4, 5.8

Assist your students in learning and using new words with this daily activity. Duplicate a copy of page 125 for each student. Each day write a new vocabulary word on the chalkboard and instruct each student to write the word on his or her chart. Discuss the pronunciation and meaning of the word. Instruct each student to create a sentence using the word and write it on the chart. Continue in this manner until the chart is completely filled.

Word of the Day

Student Directions: Record the new word of the day and complete the chart for that word.

Word of the Day	Sentence Showing How the Word Was Used

More Word-Learning Strategies

Nonsense Words

Standard: 5.4

Sometimes using context can assist in defining words even when they are nonsense words. Write the sentence below on the chalkboard and ask the students to read it silently.

- ✏ The red <u>cxoijg</u> drove down the road slowly.

Draw attention to the underlined nonsense word. Tell the students that this is not a real word, but the way it is used in the sentence might give us a clue as to what the word should be. Ask the following questions: Where is the cxoijg? What is it doing? Do you think the cxoijg is some kind of living thing? Why not? What verb gives a clue about what it is?

Lead the students to understand that the nonsense word is probably some kind of vehicle. The word *drove* and the fact that it is in the street are clues that indicate this. Continue to practice defining nonsense words using the sentences below.

- ✏ The <u>hwoei</u> sang sweetly from the treetop.
- ✏ I'm hungry for <u>sldiu</u> with chocolate syrup.
- ✏ The <u>woeih</u> blew out the candle.
- ✏ The sky was <u>woeireg</u>. There wasn't a cloud to be seen.

Multiple-Meaning Words

Standard: 5.4

Many familiar words have several meanings. For example, the word *pet* can mean "an animal that lives with people." It can also mean "a favorite" (as in "teacher's pet") or "to rub gently." By understanding that words can have more than one meaning, your students will be able to comprehend text better. See the list below for common multiple-meaning words. Then have your students complete pages 127–128 for practice.

Word	Meaning #1	Meaning #2
post	a pole	to put up
fire	flames	get rid of someone from work
shape	geometric figure	form into something
pack	put clothes in a suitcase	wolves in a group
point	tip	aim at something
corner	corner of a room	trap
spring	season	metal coil
stamp	pound the ground with foot	postage stamp
tire	wheel	wear out
shop	buy things	a store
place	a location	set down

Which Meaning?

Read each sentence. Determine the meaning of the underlined word and circle the correct definition below.

1. Be sure to <u>post</u> your message on the bulletin board.	
➤ **a pole**	➤ **to put up**
2. If I don't do a good job, the boss will <u>fire</u> me.	
➤ **flames**	➤ **get rid of someone from work**
3. Did you already <u>pack</u> for the trip?	
➤ **put clothes in a suitcase**	➤ **wolves in a group**
4. <u>Point</u> at your favorite toy.	
➤ **tip**	➤ **aim**
5. My birthday is in the <u>spring</u>.	
➤ **season**	➤ **metal coil**
6. The car has a flat <u>tire</u>.	
➤ **wheel**	➤ **wear out**
7. My sister works at the <u>shop</u> down the street.	
➤ **buy things**	➤ **a store**
8. You can <u>place</u> your books on the table.	
➤ **a location**	➤ **set down**
9. The <u>eye</u> of the hurricane hit our town.	
➤ **center**	➤ **organ used for seeing**
10. The boy gave his brother a hard <u>punch</u> in the arm.	
➤ **fruit drink**	➤ **hit**

Which Meaning? *(cont.)*

Read each sentence. Determine the meaning of the underlined word and circle the correct definition below.

---

1. I got my dad a new <u>tie</u> for his birthday.

   ➤ **fasten**   ➤ **something worn around the neck**

---

2. Raise your hand when I <u>call</u> your name.

   ➤ **use the telephone**   ➤ **say**

---

3. I planted the seeds in the flower <u>bed</u>.

   ➤ **garden**   ➤ **place to sleep**

---

4. Who is <u>running</u> for president?

   ➤ **moving quickly**   ➤ **competing**

---

5. The queen is the <u>ruler</u> of the kingdom.

   ➤ **a measuring stick**   ➤ **leader**

---

6. Be sure to <u>water</u> the flowers when the soil is dry.

   ➤ **put water on a plant**   ➤ **liquid to drink**

---

7. I heard the dog <u>bark</u> last night.

   ➤ **noise made by a dog**   ➤ **covering on a tree**

---

8. Can you give me a <u>lift</u> to the store?

   ➤ **raise**   ➤ **ride**

---

9. Would you like an <u>ear</u> of corn?

   ➤ **cob**   ➤ **organ used for hearing**

---

10. <u>Picture</u> your mom's face.

    ➤ **photograph**   ➤ **imagine**

What Do You Mean?

Directions: Determine two meanings of each word. Write two sentences using the word in different ways. The first one has been done for you.

1. **hide**

   Meaning #1: _The puppy likes to hide under the table._

   Meaning #2: _Leather is made of cow hide._

2. **slip**

   Meaning #1: _____

   Meaning #2: _____

3. **fix**

   Meaning #1: _____

   Meaning #2: _____

4. **part**

   Meaning #1: _____

   Meaning #2: _____

5. **cut**

   Meaning #1: _____

   Meaning #2: _____

6. **bowl**

   Meaning #1: _____

   Meaning #2: _____

7. **string**

   Meaning #1: _____

   Meaning #2: _____

More Word-Learning Strategies *(cont.)*

Personal Dictionary

Standard: 5.8

Learning to use the dictionary is a necessary skill. Help students understand the need for dictionaries by providing them their own mini-dictionaries filled with high-frequency words.

Materials

- copies of pages 131–137 (for each student)
- scissors
- stapler
- pencils

1. Duplicate pages 131–137 for each student.

2. Assist the students in cutting apart the pages and assembling them into booklets.

3. Review the high-frequency words on each page. Explain that a booklet filled with these words can be helpful when writing.

4. Draw students' attention to the blanks on each page and explain that these lines are provided for them to add new words that are meaningful to them.

5. Encourage the students to refer to their personal dictionaries often.

ABC Order

To effectively use dictionaries, students need to have a solid understanding of alphabetical order.

Materials: copies of pages 138–144 (for each student)

Duplicate pages 138–144 to provide practice for students with understanding alphabetical order. In this section, you will also find pages that feature the skill of identifying letters that are found at the beginning, the middle, and the end of the dictionary.

Meaningful Word Parts

Standard: 5.4, 5.6, and 5.8

Teach your students to identify word meanings by understanding the meanings of prefixes and suffixes.

Materials: copies of pages 145–146 (for each student)

Many words have prefixes and suffixes that contribute to their meaning. For example, the prefix *un* means "opposite." The opposite of "do" is "undo." The prefix *pre* means "before," so a pretest is a test that comes before another test. By reviewing the meanings of prefixes and suffixes with your students, you are providing them with skills that will help them in determining the meanings of some new words they encounter. See the list below for prefixes, suffixes, and their meanings. Have students complete pages 145–146 for additional practice.

un- = opposite	*dis-* = don't	*-ful* = having a lot of
pre- = before	*-ness* = a state of being	

Personal Dictionary

_____'s

Dictionary

A

about   _____

after   _____

again   _____

always   _____

and

_____

B

because   by

been   _____

before   _____

both   _____

bring

buy

C

came   _____

carry   _____

come   _____

could   _____

_____

_____

Personal Dictionary *(cont.)*

D

does   _____

don't   _____

done   _____

down   _____

_____

_____

E

eat   _____

eight   _____

ever   _____

every   _____

everything

_____

F

find   _____

for   _____

found   _____

four   _____

friend

funny

G

goes   _____

going   _____

good   _____

got   _____

_____

_____

Personal Dictionary *(cont.)*

H

have _____

help _____

here _____

hurt _____

_____

_____

I

into _____

it _____

its _____

_____

_____

J

jump _____

just _____

_____

_____

_____

K

keep _____

kind _____

know _____

_____

_____

Personal Dictionary *(cont.)*

L		**M**	
laugh	_____	made	_____
let	_____	make	_____
light	_____	many	_____
like	_____	most	_____
little	_____	much	
live		myself	
look			

N		**O**	
never	_____	off	_____
new	_____	once	_____
nothing	_____	one	_____
now	_____	over	_____
_____		own	
		_____	

Personal Dictionary *(cont.)*

P

play   _____

please   _____

pretty   _____

put   _____

_____

_____

Q

question   _____

quiet   _____

_____   _____

_____   _____

_____   _____

R

read   _____

ride   _____

right   _____

rope   _____

_____

_____

S

said   _____

saw   _____

say   _____

sleep   _____

some

soon

Personal Dictionary *(cont.)*

T

thank　　　_____

the　　　_____

their　　　_____

them　　　_____

there　　　_____

today

together

U

under　　　_____

upon　　　_____

us　　　_____

use　　　_____

_____

_____

V

very　　　_____

_____　_____

_____　_____

_____

_____

W

walk　　　_____

want　　　_____

wear　　　_____

were　　　_____

where

which

Personal Dictionary *(cont.)*

X	**Y**
x-ray _____	yellow _____
_____ _____	yes
_____ _____	you _____
_____	your
_____	_____

Z	**Notes**
zebra _____	_____
_____ _____	_____
_____ _____	_____
_____	_____

Beginning, Middle, or End?

Read and cut out each word below. Would the word be found at the beginning, middle, or end of the dictionary? Glue the word in the correct flower box.

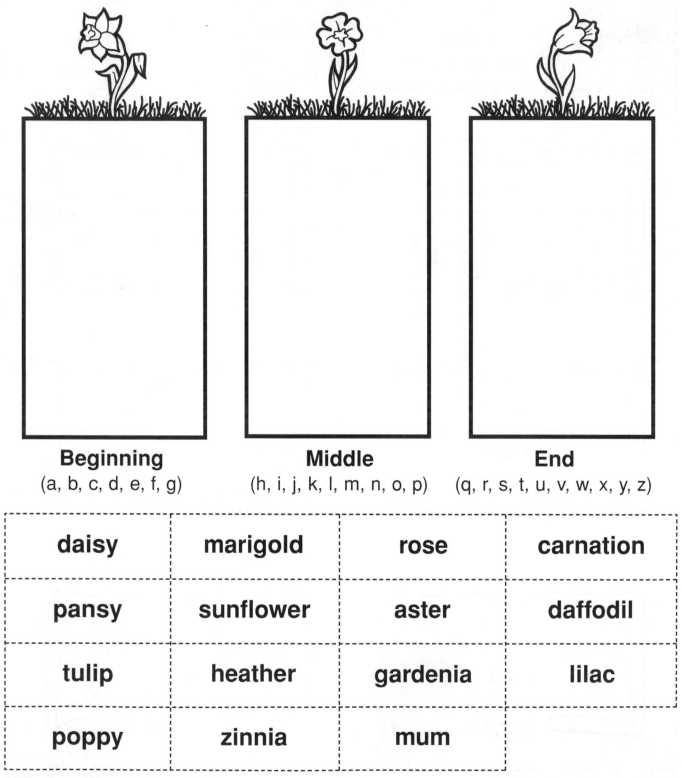

| **Beginning**
(a, b, c, d, e, f, g) | **Middle**
(h, i, j, k, l, m, n, o, p) | **End**
(q, r, s, t, u, v, w, x, y, z) |

daisy	marigold	rose	carnation
pansy	sunflower	aster	daffodil
tulip	heather	gardenia	lilac
poppy	zinnia	mum	

Using the Dictionary

Guide words at the top of dictionary pages will help you find words. The word on the left indicates the first word on that page. The word on the right indicates the last word on that page.

Directions

1. Find each word below in a dictionary.

2. Look at the top of the page that word is on to find the guide words.

3. Write the guide words on the lines at the top of each book.

arctic

polar

iceberg

frozen

sled

winter

Diggin' into the Dictionary

Directions: Answer the questions about this dictionary page below.

---

backstop	**batter**

backstop: (noun) the fence behind home plate

bad: (adjective) not good

barter: (verb) to trade

barricade: (noun) wall or barrier

baseball: (noun) a game played by hitting a ball with a bat

basement: (noun) cellar or underground room

bash: (verb) hit; (noun) party

bat: (noun) a flying mammal; (noun) a stick used to hit a ball

batter: (noun) a person who hits a ball; (noun) mix for making cake or cookies

---

1. What are the guide words on this page?_____

2. What part of speech is *baseball*? _____

3. Write a sentence using the word *barter*. _____

_____

4. What is another word for *barricade*? _____

5. How many syllables are in the word *batter*? _____

6. What is the definition of *basement*? _____

7. Write two words that are nouns. _____

8. Write a word that is an adjective. _____

Order in the Ocean!

Directios: Understanding alphabetical order makes dictionary use much easier! Put each group of words in ABC order. The first one has been done for you.

1. ocean ___ocean___

   otter ___octopus___

   octopus ___open___

   open ___otter___

2. dolphin _____

   dock _____

   diver _____

   deep _____

3. whale _____

   wave _____

   worth _____

   water _____

4. beach _____

   ball _____

   boat _____

   blue _____

5. fish _____

   forage _____

   flounder _____

   fin _____

6. starfish _____

   sea _____

   snail _____

   sail _____

7. crab _____

   catfish _____

   coral _____

   clownfish _____

8. bay _____

   blowhole _____

   barracuda _____

   barnacle _____

Raging Raceway

Write these words in alphabetical order on the racecars below and on page 143.

yellow	ice	put	very
able	open	read	x-ray
when	filling	jump	quit
cap	love	town	hollow
eel	box	down	zoo
sigh	new	use	many
goat	keep		

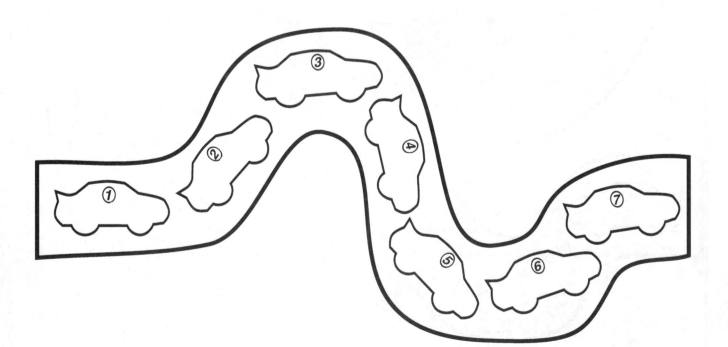

Raging Raceway *(cont.)*

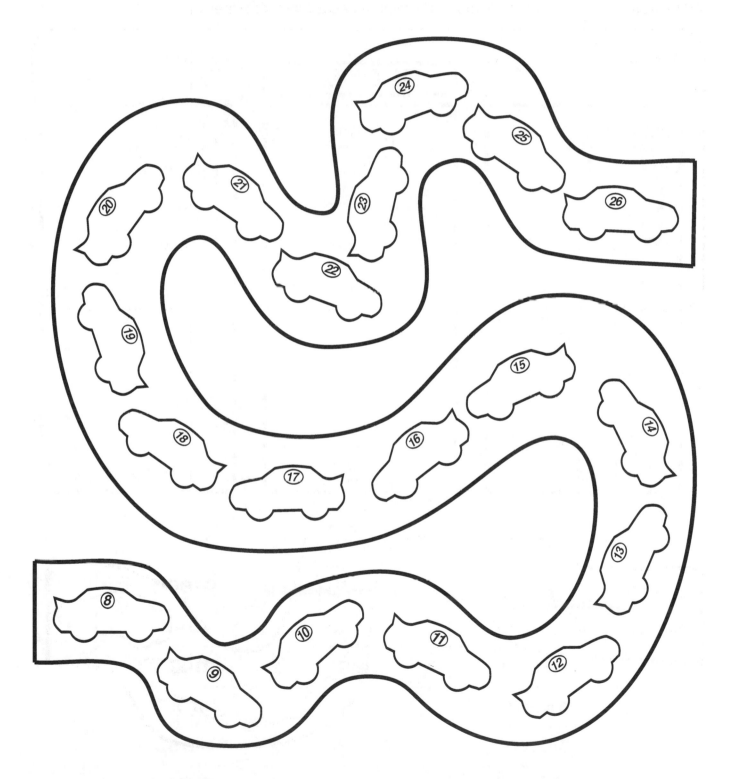

City Skyline

Directions: Read the words below. Cut out the words and glue them in alphabetical order on the correct building.

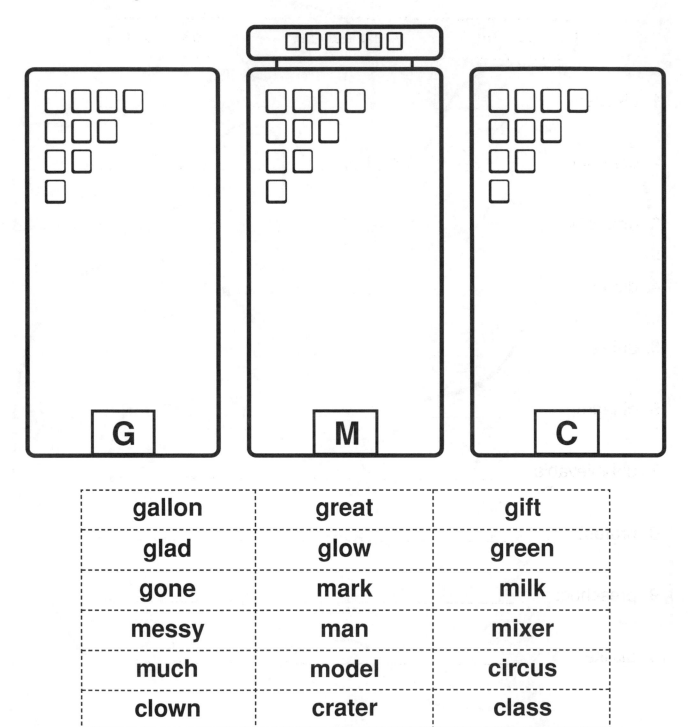

gallon	great	gift
glad	glow	green
gone	mark	milk
messy	man	mixer
much	model	circus
clown	crater	class
cabbage	cup	courage

Prefixes

Directions: See the meanings of the prefixes below. Write the meaning of each word. Use the list below to help you. The first two have been answered for you.

> • *un* = not　　　• *pre* = before　　　• *dis* = don't

1. disobey　　　_don't obey_

2. prejudge　　　_judge before_

3. unhappy　　　_____

4. disable　　　_____

5. unlike　　　_____

6. disagree　　　_____

7. unbelievable　　　_____

8. pretest　　　_____

9. preschool　　　_____

10. dislike　　　_____

Suffixes

Directions: See the meanings of the suffixes below. Write the meaning of each word. Use the list below to help you. The first few have been done for you.

> • *ness* = a state of being   • *ful* = having a lot of

1. sadness   being sad

2. delightful   having a lot of delight

3. wonderful   _____

4. careful   _____

5. happiness   _____

6. softness   _____

7. colorful   _____

8. joyful   _____

9. loneliness   _____

10. harmful   _____

Comprehension

What is reading without understanding? Reading is, first and foremost, a meaning-making process. Without comprehension, reading is not reading.

➤ **Purpose**—Reading is about purpose. We read to locate information. We read for enjoyment. Good readers know that the process of reading involves purpose.

➤ **Thinking**—Good readers think as they read. They concentrate on storyline, vocabulary, and they focus on making sense of text.

Why Is Comprehension Instruction Important?

According to the National Reading Panel's report, research suggests that instruction of comprehension strategies helps children to become more purposeful, active readers. They make use of prior knowledge to connect new information with information that is already known as well as using visual images to form mental pictures that make written material more meaningful. Effective instruction in this area involves the following:

1. **Monitoring**

2. **Using Graphic Organizers**

3. **Answering Questions**

4. **Generating Questions**

5. **Recognizing Story Structure**

6. **Summarizing**

---

1. Monitoring Comprehension

There are many ways that students can monitor their own comprehension, including the following:

- identifying unfamiliar words
- identifying information that is not understood
- clarifying new understandings
- reviewing information featured in text
- searching for clarifying information in text

2. Graphic Organizers

Graphic or semantic organizers are visual representations of concepts and ideas. These can be in the form of maps, webs, clusters, charts, and graphs. Graphic organizers assist readers with:

- identifying a purpose for reading
- organizing thoughts about written information

Comprehension *(cont.)*

3. Answering Questions

Questioning strategies are helpful in the development of comprehension. By using questioning strategies, teachers can effectively monitor their students' comprehension. Questioning assists in the following ways:

- providing purpose for reading
- focusing students' attention on meaning
- encouraging thinking while reading
- reviewing what was read

4. Generating Questions

Comprehension can also be increased by teaching children to ask their own questions about text. When generating questions about text, students use metacognitive strategies that confirm the things they do and do not understand when reading.

5. Recognizing Story Structure

When students understand story structure, they have knowledge of how events are organized to form the plot of a story. This knowledge leads to better story recall and understanding. Instruction in this area involves:

- setting
- events
- characters
- plot

Story maps and other kinds of graphic organizers can be used with instruction on story structure to clarify story content.

6. Summarizing

When students summarize stories, they must have enough understanding about a piece of text to condense the main ideas to just a few sentences. Summarizing involves the use of the following skills:

- identifying main ideas
- connecting ideas
- removing insignificant details
- story recall

This section of the book provides activities that focus on monitoring, questioning, generating questions, using graphic organizers, understanding story structure, and summarizing. In addition to these, you will find tools for comprehension assessment.

Monitoring Comprehension

What Do You Know?

Metacognition refers to the ability to think about one's thinking. This is an important skill for readers to learn. A good reader understands not only what is known, but also what is unknown. You can assist your children with their metacognitive skills by doing the following:

1. When a student asks for help with an assignment, ask the child what it is that he or she does not understand. Rather than saying, "I don't understand this," the student might say, "I don't understand the directions," or "I don't know the meaning of this word." Encouraging each student to pinpoint the area of misunderstanding will assist him or her to become a better reader.

2. When questioning students about information from a story, ask higher-order questions that require them to analyze information and events, come up with new ideas, and offer opinions. In addition to this, have the students create questions whose answers would help to clarify information.

Reality vs. Fantasy

Standard: 6.1

Being able to differentiate reality from fantasy is an important skill for young readers. The stories listed below are great examples of both reality and fantasy. As you read these stories aloud to your students, encourage them to comment on events that could or could not really happen. As a follow-up activity, instruct each student to fold a sheet of paper in half and label the halves: **Reality** and **Fantasy**. On one side, the student illustrates an event from the story that represents something real. On the other side, the student illustrates an event from the story that represents something that is a fantasy. To continue practice of this skill, duplicate page 150 for each child to complete.

Reality/Fantasy Books

Sharmat, Marjorie Weinman. *Gila Monsters Meet You at the Airport.* Scott Foresman, 1990.

Van Allsburg, Chris. *Jumanji.* Houghton Mifflin Co., 1981.

Munsch, Robert. *Pigs.* Annick Press, 1992.

Kellogg, Steven. *Can I Keep Him?* Puffin, 1992.

Numeroff, Laura Joffe. *If You Give a Mouse a Cookie.* Laura Geringer, 1985.

Sequencing Events

Standard: 6.1, 6.2

You can monitor your students' understanding of a story by asking them to sequence information. This can be done in many ways.

1. Ask students to name events that happened in a story they've read. Write their responses on chart paper. Then have students work together to number the events in the order they happened in the story.

2. Write a different story event on each of several sentence strips. Display the events in random order in a pocket chart. As a learning center activity, have students work with partners to place the sentence strips in the correct sequence.

3. Duplicate and distribute the sequencing reproducible on page 151 for students to complete.

Reality vs. Fantasy

Directions: Read each sentence. Color each animal according to this code:

Coloring Code

Reality → Color the animal.   Fantasy → Don't color the animal.

1. The cat sang a song.

2. Lizards watch television.

3. Some snakes eat mice.

4. Kittens are soft.

5. Fish need clean water.

6. Hamsters are good at math.

7. Some parrots can talk.

8. Mice are smaller than dogs.

9. Turtles are great surfers.

10. Chameleons can change colors.

Sequencing Events

Directions: Read the story. Then cut and paste the events below in proper order.

On the night before her family vacation, Tracy began packing. She needed clothes that would keep her warm in the mountains. Tracy packed a coat and many warm sweaters. Then she packed some long pants, socks, and boots. Finally, Tracy packed some cozy pajamas. Just as she was ready to zip up her suitcase, she remembered her journal! She wanted to write about every detail of her vacation. As Tracy lay on her bed thinking of her exciting trip, she drifted off to sleep.

1.

2.

3.

4.

5.

Tracy packed her journal.

Tracy packed her coat.

She packed her socks.

Tracy fell asleep.

She packed her pajamas.

Graphic Organizers

On Display

Standards: 6.2, 6.4, 7.2

Graphic organizers are useful for displaying information in a visual way. The use of graphic organizers helps students to organize information and increase understanding. See the graphic organizers and descriptions below.

✏ Story Map

A story map can be used to display the sequence of events in a story. When teaching your students how to use a story map, enlist their help (as a group) to map the events of a story read to the class. Post a large sheet of bulletin-board paper or chart paper for all to see. Then begin by drawing a circle or a square. The first event of the story is written inside the shape. (Ask the students to offer their ideas for the events to be written on the map.) Draw an arrow following the shape, then draw another shape and write the next story event inside it. Continue in this manner until the map is complete. (See the illustration for an example.) You can also provide a flow chart (page 155) for students to create their own story maps.

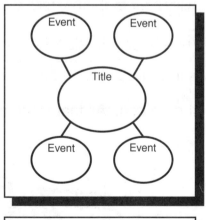

✏ Word Web

A word web is a great tool for organizing ideas. You can use a word web to record events from a story or attributes of a story character. (See the illustration.) Display a large web on bulletin-board paper or chart paper. To make a character web, write the name of the character in the center circle. In each of the surrounding circles, write a different character trait. Be sure to allow the students to suggest the words or phrases to be written in each section of the web. Duplicate page 154 for each student and have them create their own word webs.

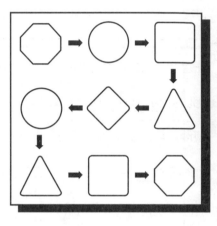

✏ Charts

Charts can be used in a variety of ways to assist children with their comprehension. For example, you can create a chart of questions for students to complete as they read a story. You can also have students compare and identify information about characters by completing a story chart. See the example to the right for a way to use a story chart.

Farmer Gray's Morning

Directions

1. Read the story below.

2. Complete the web on page 154 by writing the title of the story in the center circle and the main events in the surrounding circles.

3. Complete the flow chart on page 155 by writing the first event that takes place in the story in the first box. Follow the arrow to the next box and write the next event that takes place there. Continue until you've written every event that happens in the story.

Farmer Gray woke up as the sun was rising. He had a lot of work to do. He went outside and looked at the sky. A storm was brewing in the distance. He knew he needed to hurry. So, he went to the barn and gave fresh hay to the horses. He cleaned the pigpen and fed the chickens. He checked the hen house and collected the eggs from the nests. He ran inside and put the eggs in the refrigerator. Then he hiked out to the pasture to check on the cows. As Farmer Gray headed back to the house, the sky grew dark and it started to rain. He made it to the house as the storm showered down on him. He opened the door and smelled eggs and bacon cooking in the kitchen. All that work, and the day had only just begun!

Web

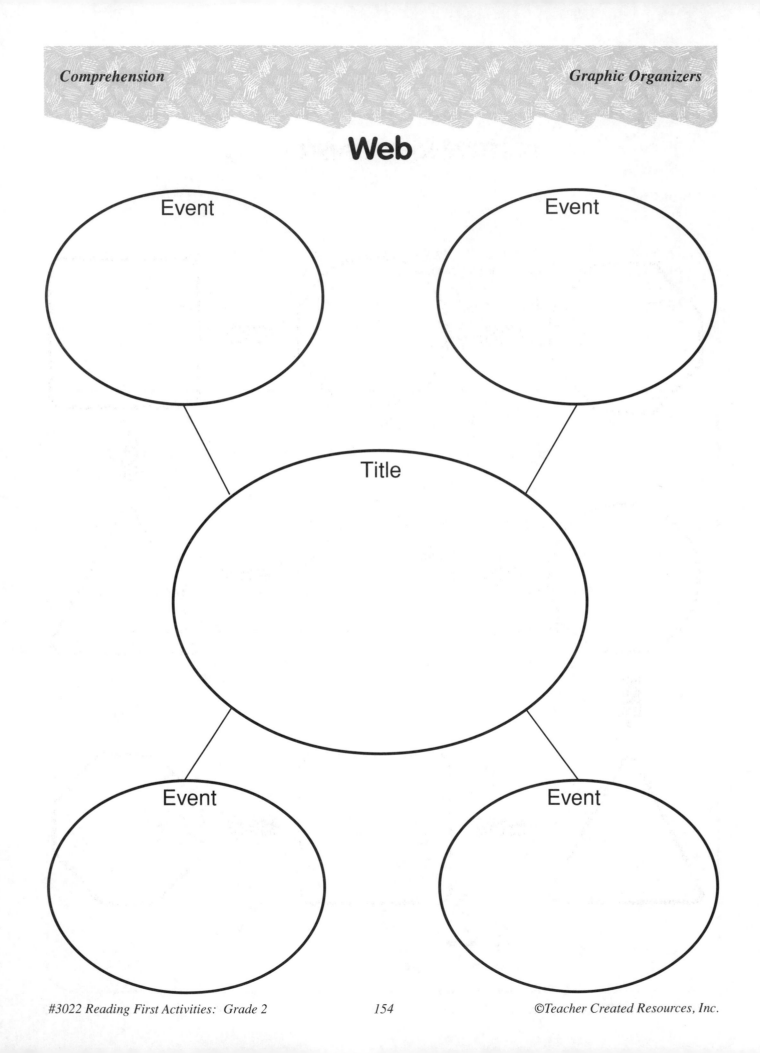

Event

Event

Title

Event

Event

Flow Chart

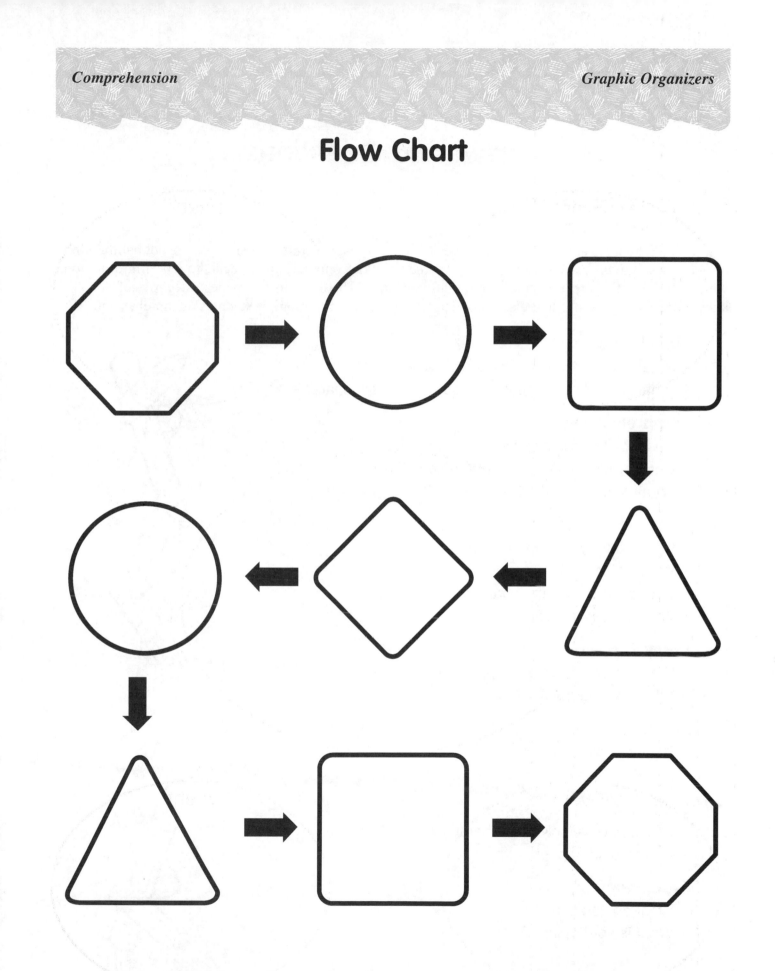

Answering Questions

Questioning Strategies

Standard: 6.1, 6.2, 6.3, 6.4

Questioning students about their understanding of a story is something most educators do, but the kind of questions asked is extremely important. Some questions only require students to repeat information, while other questions require students to think critically. The list below provides categories of knowledge with questions and discussion-starters you can use to monitor students' comprehension.

✏ **Knowledge**
- What events do you recall from the story?
- What traits do you remember about the main character?

✏ **Comprehension**
- Describe the story setting.
- Compare two characters in the story.
- What is the main idea of the story?

✏ **Application**
- What conclusion can be drawn about . . . ?
- What evidence is given about . . . ?
- Why do you think the character did that?
- Write an example of . . .

✏ **Analysis**
- What do you think will happen next?
- What caused that to happen?

✏ **Synthesis**
- Design a plan for . . .
- Develop a way the character could . . .

✏ **Construct**
- How could we solve the character's problem?
- What would happen if . . . ?

✏ **Evaluation**
- What do you think?
- What is your opinion?

The Secret

Directions: Read the story and answer the questions.

Vanessa and Chloe woke up early on Saturday morning. "Mom is still asleep, I think," Vanessa whispered. "Maybe if we hurry, we can finish before she wakes up," replied Chloe. The girls tiptoed to the living room and pulled a large box from behind the couch. "Did you get the paper?" asked Vanessa. Chloe handed her the roll of bright red, yellow, and orange paper. "She's going to love this, don't you think?" Chloe smiled and said, "This will really help her in the garden." The girls finished wrapping the box and slid it behind the couch again. They heard some noises down the hallway and then quickly jumped on the couch and pretended to be looking at books. "Girls," mother said, "what are you up to?" "Nothing, Mom," they replied.

1. Who are Vanessa and Chloe? How do you know? _____

_____

2. Why were they whispering? _____

_____

3. What was special about this day? _____

_____

4. How do you think Mom feels about gardening? _____

_____

5. What do you think was inside the box? _____

_____

6. Why do you think the girls didn't give the box to Mom? _____

_____

Generating Questions

Literature Circles

Standard: 5.9, 6.1, 6.2, 6.3, 6.5

Literature circles are a great way for children to generate questions about the stories they are reading.

Materials: several copies of the same children's book, several packs of adhesive notes

1. Place students into groups of three or four.
2. Provide each student in the group with the same book to read and a pack of adhesive notes.
3. Instruct the students to read the story (on his or her own) and think about questions they have about the story line, the characters, the setting, etc.
4. Each time a child thinks of a question, have him or her write it down on an adhesive note and attach it to the page that relates to the question.
5. Encourage the students to generate critical-thinking questions by providing a list of question starters (see below).
6. After each child in the group has finished reading the book, have them meet to discuss the story and ask their questions.

Critical-Thinking Question Starters

- ✏ What do you think . . .?
- ✏ Why do you think [this event] happened?

- ✏ I wonder . . .?
- ✏ Have you ever thought about . . .?

- ✏ What would have happened if . . .?
- ✏ What would you do if [this event] happened to you?

- ✏ What is your opinion about . . .?
- ✏ Can you figure out why [this character] did . . .?

Be a Reporter

Standard: 6.2

Have some fun with question-generating by having your students imagine that they are reporters. Instruct them to think of questions they would ask the main character of a story they have recently read. Have students use the form on page 159 to get them started. After generating these questions, designate other students to pretend to be the character and allow them to have a question/answer session. After this session, instruct students to use the information they gathered to write news stories to present to the class. You might consider combining the articles into a class newspaper to share with parents.

Comprehension Game Board

Standards: 6.1, 6.2, 6.4

This activity will help your students to reflect their understanding of a story. Duplicate pages 160 and 161 for each student to assemble into a game board. The student then writes questions about the story on index cards. When students have completed their game boards and question cards, have them trade games with other students to check their comprehension.

Question Planning

Use this page to assist you with generating questions about a book you have read.

1. Write your questions about something you wonder about the main character.

   _____

   _____

   _____

   _____

2. Did the story leave you wondering about something? Write your questions below.

   _____

   _____

   _____

   _____

3. Think about where the story took place. Write some questions about this location.

   _____

   _____

   _____

   _____

4. If a friend of yours read this book, what would you like to ask him or her about the story?
   Write your questions below. _____

   _____

   _____

   _____

5. If you could meet the author of this story, what would you like to ask him or her? Write
   your questions below._____

   _____

   _____

   _____

Comprehension Game

Directions (for two players)

1. Place a game marker on **START.**

2. Player 1 draws a card and answers the question. If correct, the student moves ahead one space. If incorrect, the student does not move ahead.

3. Player 2 takes a turn in the same way.

4. Players alternate turns.

5. The player who reaches **FINISH** first wins the game.

Comprehension Game (cont.)

Story-Structure Activities

Details, Details, Details

Standard: 6.2

This activity assists your children with the identification of story details.

Materials

- drawing paper
- crayons or markers
- passage of text (with lots of detail)

1. Distribute a sheet of drawing paper to each student.

2. Read aloud a passage of text or a short story that contains quite a bit of detail.

3. Instruct each student to draw a picture of something in the story and emphasize the details described by the author.

4. After completing the drawings, allow students to share them with one another, explaining why he or she included certain details in the drawing.

Group Stories

Standard: 6.2

By participating in this fun activity, your students will practice implementing what they know about story structure.

1. Gather the students together in a circle and explain that they will be creating a group story. Remind them that stories have specific characters, settings, and events. Remind them also that there are events that happen at the beginning, middle, and end of the story and that these events are interrelated.

2. Tell the students that they must listen carefully to the information contributed by other classmates so that they can create a story that is clear and organized.

3. Begin the story by stating the setting and main character. (You could also designate a student to begin the story.)

4. Another student takes over the story and adds an event or description.

5. Continue in this manner until all students have had the chance to contribute to the story.

6. Take time to review the completed story, identifying the main characters, setting, and beginning, middle, and ending events.

7. To make this activity even more interesting, fill a bag with different small objects (such as a leaf, a ball, a key, a handkerchief, etc.). As students are telling their portions of the story, periodically hand the bag to a student and ask him or her to reach in and take out an object. The object selected must then be included in the story in some way.

Story-Structure Activities *(cont.)*

Postcard to a Character

Standard: 6.2

This activity will assist your students in thinking about the traits of a character in a story.

Materials

- children's book
- paper
- pencils
- copy of page 164 (for each student)
- crayons or markers

1. Read aloud a story with a strong main character.
2. Discuss the story and have the students talk about the main character's personality and actions.
3. Have the students think about what they might like to say to the character if they were able to meet him or her.
4. Instruct the students to write down their ideas.
5. Distribute student copies of the postcard pattern on page 164 and have each student use the information on his or her paper to write a postcard to the character.
6. As a class, create a make-believe address that can be written on the postcard.
7. Encourage each student to color a picture on the back of the postcard.
8. Display the completed postcards for all to see.

Setting Dioramas

Standard: 6.2

Give your students the opportunity to focus in on the setting of a story with this project.

Materials

- 13" x 13" square of construction paper
- scissors
- construction paper scraps (assorted colors)
- markers or crayons
- glue
- copy of page 165 (for each student)

1. Assist the children in making the diorama "stage." Give each student a cut-out copy of the square on page 165. Begin by folding the paper square diagonally to make a triangle. Crease the fold.
2. Open the square back up and fold diagonally in the opposite direction. There will now be a criss-cross fold on the open square.
3. Cut on the fold line from one of the corners to the center of the square. (Do not cut any further than the center.)
4. Take the two flaps on either side of the cut line and overlap them. A triangular shape "stage" will be the result. Glue the overlapping flaps together.
5. Have each student use construction paper, markers or crayons, and glue to recreate the setting of the story.

Postcard Pattern

Diorama Pattern

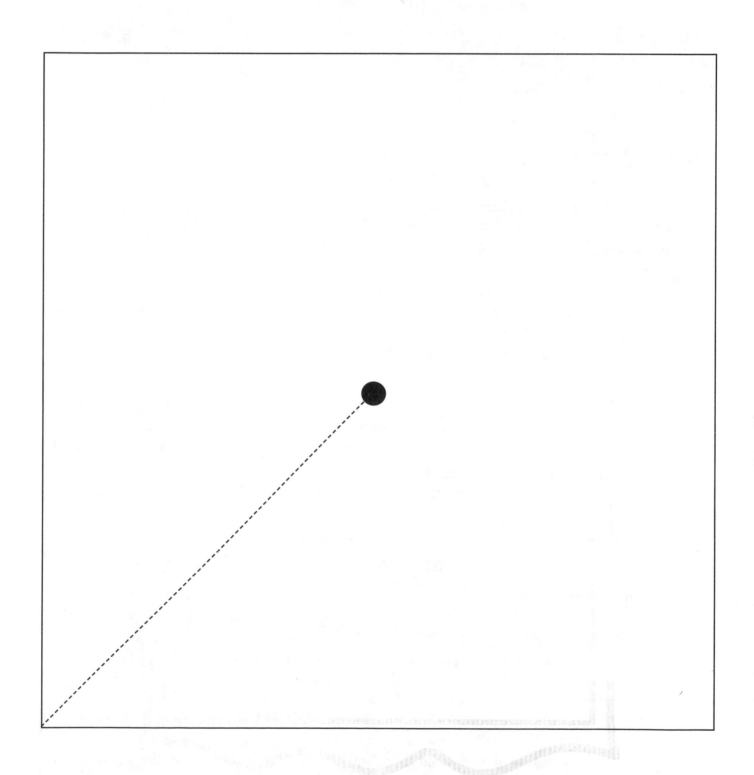

More Story-Structure Activities

The following activity helps your students identify specific events in a story.

Story Pyramid

Standard: 6.2

Materials

- chart paper
- marker
- paper
- children's story
- pencils

1. Discuss with your students different elements of a story:

   ➣ main character   ➣ problem   ➣ setting   ➣ solution

2. Display a few familiar children's books and ask the students to identify the problem that happened in each one. Then explain that solving the problem in the story often involves several steps.

3. Read a short children's story and ask the students to think about the problem in the story and how it was solved.

4. On a sheet of chart paper, draw the organizer below. Ask the students to identify the information that needs to be added to the web, including the three steps that took place in the story to lead to the solution.

5. For additional practice, have students draw their own organizers to complete with information from stories of their choice.

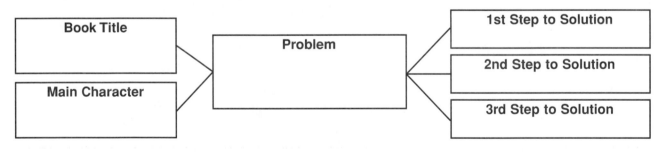

Additional Activities

✐ Direct students to draw pictures of characters or creatures in the story. Use the cutouts to develop a theme-related bulletin board. For an ocean bulletin board, create embellishments by having students cut out sand-castle shapes from sandpaper.

✐ Have students make dioramas in shoeboxes showing the setting. Encourage the students to use the illustrations in the book to gain ideas for the diorama. If, for instance, you are using the book *Commotion in the Ocean* by Giles Andreae, have students attach blue cellophane to the insides of the box and glue sand to the bottom of the box. Instruct students to cut out construction-paper ocean creatures.

✐ Divide students into small groups and have them develop plays based on parts of the book. Allow ample time for rehearsal and then schedule a day to perform plays for the class.

Story Chart

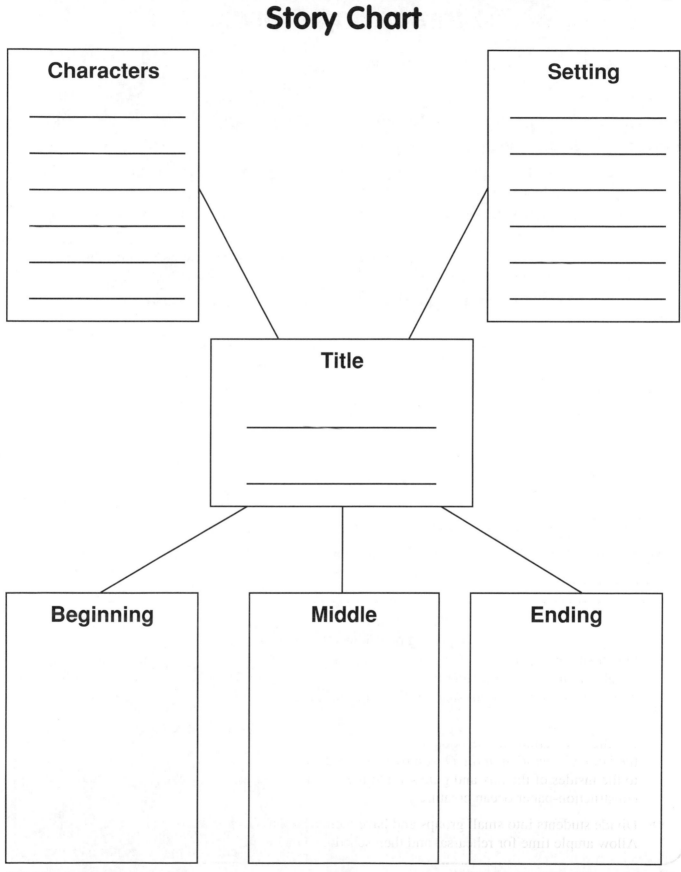

Characters

_____

_____

_____

_____

_____

_____

Setting

_____

_____

_____

_____

_____

_____

Title

_____

_____

Beginning

Middle

Ending

Summarizing Activities

Main Idea

Standard: 6.4

Use this activity to help your students practice the process of identifying the main idea of a story.

Materials: chalkboard and chalk, passage of text or a children's short story

1. Begin the lesson by telling your students a story about a recent event in your life. After telling the story, ask the students to retell the events they remember.

2. Draw an idea web on the chalkboard. Ask the students to think about the general idea of the story. What was it about?

3. Explain that this is called the *main idea* and write it in the center of the web. Have the children name supporting details from the story as you write them in the surrounding circles on the web.

4. Read a passage of text to the class or have the students read it themselves. Ask them to identify the main idea.

5. To assist your children with differentiating the main idea from the supporting events, select a sentence from the story. Ask them, "Is the story all about this one fact?"

6. Continue in this manner until the main idea has been identified.

7. Review that the main idea of a story is the one thing that all the other events support.

Insignificant Details

Standard: 6.4

This activity helps your students to separate important details from insignificant details.

Materials: passage of text or children's short story, chart paper, marker

1. Explain to the students that when telling the main idea of a story, it is necessary to include important details. Some details are important to include. Some details are not as important and are only used to provide additional information or description.

2. Have the students read a passage of text.

3. Check for comprehension by asking questions relating to the story.

4. Have the students name things they can remember as you write their responses on chart paper. Then review each sentence.

5. First, identify the sentence that represents the main idea.

6. Then review the remaining sentences to determine whether each detail is important in explaining the main idea or whether it is insignificant.

Irrelevant Details

Standard: 6.4

Have your students practice identifying irrelevant information by completing page 169. To complete the page, each student reads each passage of text and finds the one sentence that does not make sense.

Irrelevant Details

Read each paragraph. Find the sentence that does not fit with the rest of the sentences.
Draw a line through it.

1. Katie studied very hard for the spelling test. She wrote each word 10 times and then tried to spell each word without looking. She was ready! She wore a red dress to school. Then the test began, but Katie got nervous. Would she remember how to spell the words?

2. It was the day of the school parade. The children were dressed in costumes. The floats were ready to go. All of the parents were gathered along the sidewalks. I can't wait for Christmas.

3. The air grew cold as the storm rolled in. The sky was cloudy and dark. Shelly's new dog ate breakfast. Thunder could be heard in the distance. Shelly decided she had better take an umbrella with her to school.

4. Planting a flower garden is easy and fun. Daisies are pretty. All you need is a plot of dirt, some seeds, and water. First, you make several small holes in the dirt. Then you sprinkle a few seeds in each hole and cover them with dirt. Just water the garden when it's dry, and in a few weeks your garden will begin to grow!

5. Have you ever been to a circus? I love to see all of the animals do tricks. The elephants look smart, and the dancing bears are so cute. I love to watch the man on the trapeze. That looks scary. I wonder if I can go get pizza after the show.

6. David's cat had six kittens. They were born early in the morning before the sun came up. There are two black ones, two white ones, one orange one, and one gray. They still have their eyes closed and they make tiny little mewing sounds. Lea had a cat when she was little, but it ran away.

More Summarizing Activities

Writing a Summary

Standard: 7.3

Help your students to summarize stories with this lesson.

Materials: chalkboard and chalk

1. Explain that sometimes it is necessary to tell about a story using only a few sentences. This is called *summarizing*. For example, if you went on a vacation to Disneyland, there would be a lot of things to talk about. If you were to tell someone about your trip, you might find it necessary to tell about the vacation by summarizing the important highlights of the trip.

2. Write the following sentences on the chalkboard and review them with the students:
   - My family went to Disneyland.
   - We went to the haunted house.
   - We rode on the teacups.
   - We snacked on chocolate-covered bananas.
   - We also ate a big lunch in Tomorrowland.
   - At night we saw the light parade.
   - I was so tired that I fell asleep on the drive home.

3. Next, ask students to think of a way to tell about this trip using only two or three sentences.
   - My family went to Disneyland. We went on a lot of rides and ate good food.

Paraphrasing

Standard: 7.3

Practice with paraphrasing will help your students to better summarize stories.

Materials: children's short story

1. Review with the students the meaning of *summarizing*. Remind them that when a story is summarized, it is retold using just a few sentences. Summarizing involves telling the main idea of the story and few important details. For example, if we summarize the story "Cinderella," we might say:

   Cinderella had a mean family. They made her do all of the work. Then she went to a party and met a prince. They fell in love, and she didn't have to live with her family anymore.

2. Draw students' attention to the fact that only four sentences were used to retell the story.

3. Then explain to students that when we retell a story, we don't use the exact words of the author. We use our own words. This is called *paraphrasing*.

4. Practice paraphrasing as a group by reading aloud a story and then allowing students to offer their paraphrased summaries. (If students use exact words from the story, assist them in changing the words.)

Assessment

Track student progress by recording comments about comprehension several times throughout the year.

Student: _____   Date: _____

General Comprehension

_____

_____

Answering Comprehension Questions

_____

_____

Generating Comprehension Questions

_____

_____

Using Graphic Organizers for Comprehension

_____

_____

_____

Understanding Story Structure

_____

_____

_____

Summarizing

_____

_____

_____

Additional Comments

_____

_____

_____

Self-Assessment

Answer the questions to check your comprehension as you read a story.

1. Who are the main characters? _____
   _____

2. Describe one of the characters (personality and appearance).
   _____

   _____

3. What is the setting of the story? _____
   _____

4. What happened at the beginning? _____
   _____

5. What was the problem in the story? _____
   _____

6. How was the problem resolved? _____
   _____

7. How did the story end? _____
   _____

8. What part of the story did you enjoy the most? _____
   _____

9. List two questions that you have about the story line or the
   characters. _____

   _____

   _____

   _____

Answer Key

Page 28
1. cup
2. wiggle
3. riddle
4. chap
5. silk
6. rag
7. ticket
8. cake
9. low
10. brown

Page 42

leak	seal	bead
treat	wheel	feet
seat	jeans	meat

Page 44

candy	baby	bunny
key	forty	money
fly	cherry	eye

Page 46
1. hard
2. soft
3. hard
4. hard
5. soft
6. hard
7. hard
8. hard
9. soft
10. hard
11. hard
12. hard
13. soft
14. hard

Page 47
1. soft
2. hard
3. soft
4. soft
5. hard
6. soft
7. hard
8. hard
9. hard
10. hard
11. soft
12. hard
13. soft
14. hard

Page 48
1. staircase
2. mailbox
3. spaceship
4. raincoat
5. football
6. rainbow
7. starfish
8. eyeball
9. bowtie

Page 54
1. es
2. s
3. es
4. es
5. s
6. es
7. s
8. es
9. es
10. s
11. s
12. es

Page 58
1. town
2. clown
3. out
4. shout
5. boil
6. spoil
7. boy
8. toy
9. how
10. cow
11. toil
12. oil
13. oyster
14. loud

Page 61

h <u>ow</u>	c <u>ow</u>
n <u>ow</u>	y <u>ou</u>
pl <u>ow</u>	t <u>ow</u>
r <u>ow</u>	l <u>ou</u> d
sh <u>ou</u> t	r <u>ou</u> nd
c <u>oi</u> n	t <u>ow</u> n
<u>oi</u> nk	n <u>ou</u> n
ch <u>oi</u> ce	j <u>oy</u>
s <u>oy</u>	b <u>oy</u>
t <u>oy</u>	<u>oy</u> ster

Page 120
1. No Slang
2. Slang
3. Slang
4. No Slang
5. Slang
6. Slang
7. Slang
8. No Slang
9. Slang
10. Slang
11. No Slang
12. No Slang

Answer Key

Page 127
1. to put up
2. get rid of someone from work
3. put clothes in a suitcase
4. aim
5. season
6. wheel
7. a store
8. set down
9. center
10. hit

Page 128
1. something worn around the neck
2. say
3. garden
4. competing
5. leader
6. put water on a plant
7. noise made by a dog
8. ride
9. cob
10. imagine

Page 138
Beginning:
daisy
carnation
aster
daffodil
Middle:
marigold
pansy
heather
gardenia
lilac
poppy
mum
End:
rose
sunflower
tulip
zinnia

Page 140
1. *backstop* and *batter*
2. noun
3. Answers will vary.
4. *wall* or *barrier*
5. two
6. cellar or underground room
7. Answers will vary.
8. bad

Page 141
1. ocean, octopus, open, otter
2. deep, diver, dock, dolphin
3. water, wave, whale, worth
4. ball, beach, blue, boat
5. fin, fish, flounder, forage
6. sail, sea, snail, starfish
7. catfish, clownfish, coral, crab
8. barnacle, barracuda, bay, blowhole

Page 142
1. able
2. box
3. cap
4. down
5. eel
6. filling
7. goat
8. hollow
9. ice
10. jump
11. keep
12. love
13. many
14. new
15. open
16. put
17. quit
18. read
19. sigh
20. town
21. use
22. very
23. when
24. x-ray
25. yellow
26. zoo

Page 144
g:
gallon
gift
glad
glow
gone
great
green
m:
man
mark
messy
milk
mixer
model
much
c:
cabbage
circus
class
clown
courage
crater
cup

Page 145
3. not happy
4. don't be able
5. not like
6. don't agree
7. not believable
8. test before the test

9. school before school

10. don't like

Page 146

3. having a lot of wonder

4. havinf a lot of care

5. being happy

6. being soft

7. having a lot of color

8. having a lot of joy

9. being lonely

10. having a lot of harm

Page 150

1. no color

2. no color

3. color

4. color

5. color

6. no color

7. color

8. color

9. no color

10. color

Page 151

1. Tracy packed her coat.

2. She packed her socks.

3. She packed her pajamas.

4. Tracy packed her journal.

5. Tracy fell asleep.

Page 157

1. They are sisters. They woke up in the same house and talked about "Mom."

2. Mom was sleeping.

3. Answers may vary, but it was probably Mom's birthday.

4. She probably enjoys it.

5. It was probably some kind of garden tool.

6. Answers will vary.

Page 169

1. She wore a red dress to school.

2. I can't wait for Christmas.

3. Shelly's new dog ate breakfast.

4. Daisies are pretty.

5. I wonder if I can go get pizza after the show.

6. Lea had a cat when she was little, but it ran away.

References

Nonfiction

Center for the Improvement of Early Reading Achievement (2001). *Put Reading First.* U.S. Department of Education.

Bader, Lois A. *Bader Reading and Language Inventory and Readers Passages Pkg. (4th Edition).* Prentice Hall, 2001.

Burns, Paul C. and Betty D. Roe. *Informal Reading Inventory: Preprimer to Twelfth Grade.* Houghton Mifflin, 2002.

Goodman, Yetta M. *Reading Miscue Inventory: Alternative Procedures.* Richard C. Owen Publishing, 1987.

Johns, Jerry. *Basic Reading Inventory, 8th edition (including CD-Rom).* Kendall/Hunt Publishing Company, 2001.

Leslie, Lauren and Joanne Caldwell. *Qualitative Reading Inventory.* HarperCollins College Division, 1994.

Leslie, Lauren and Joanne Caldwell. *Qualitative Reading Inventory-3 (3rd Edition).* Pearson Allyn & Bacon, 2000.

Manzo, Anthony V. *Informal Reading-Thinking Inventory.* Wadsworth Publishing, 1995.

Scott, Janet M. and Sheila C. McCleary. *Diagnostic Reading Inventory for Primary & Intermediate Grades.* Scott & McCleary, 1993.

Silvaroli, Nicholas. *Classroom Reading Inventory.* McGraw-Hill, 2000.

References

Fiction

Ahlberg, Janet. *Each Peach Pear Plum.* Scholastic, 1981.

Andreae, Giles. *Commotion in the Ocean.* Tiger Tales, 2002.

Barrett, Judi. *Animals Should Definitely Not Wear Clothing.* Aladdin Library, 1988.

Carle, Eric. *The Very Hungry Caterpillar.* Putnam Pub Group, 1983.

Christelow, Eileen. *Five Little Monkeys Jumping on the Bed.* Houghton Mifflin Co., 1998.

Gag, Wanda. *Millions of Cats.* Paper Star, 1996.

Geddes, Anne. *10 in the Bed.* Andrews McMeel Publishing, 2001.

Hoberman, Mary Ann. *A House is a House for Me.* Viking Press, 1978.

Hutchins, Pat. *Rosie's Walk.* Scott Foresman, 1971.

Kalan, Robert. *Jump, Frog, Jump.* William Morrow, 1995.

Keats, Ezra. *Over in the Meadow.* Puffin, 1999.

Kellogg, Steven. *Can I Keep Him?* Puffin, 1992.

Martin, Bill Jr. *Brown Bear, Brown Bear, What Do You See?* Henry Holt & Company, Inc., 1996.

Martin, Bill Jr. *Chicka Chicka Boom Boom.* Aladdin Library, 2000.

Munsch, Robert. *50 Below Zero.* Annick Press, 1992.

Munsch, Robert. *Pigs.* Annick Press, 1992.

Numeroff, Laura Joffe. *If You Give a Mouse a Cookie.* Laura Geringer, 1985.

Raffi. *Wheels on the Bus: Raffi Songs to Read.* Crown Publishing Group, 1998.

Rosen, Michael. *We're Going on a Bear Hunt.* Aladdin Library, 2003.

Sharmat, Marjorie Weinman. *Gila Monsters Meet You at the Airport.* Scott Foresman, 1990.

Shaw, Charles G. *It Looked Like Spilt Milk.* HarperCollins Juvenile Books, 1947.

Shaw, Nancy. *Sheep in a Jeep.* Houghton Mifflin Co., 1988.

Stevens, Janet. *The House that Jack Built.* Holiday House, 1985.

Van Allsburg, Chris. *Jumanji.* Houghton Mifflin Co., 1981.

Viorst, Judith. *Alexander and the Terrible, Horrible, No Good, Very Bad Day.* Aladdin Library, 1987.

Wood, Audrey. *The Napping House.* Harcourt, 1984.

Wood, Audrey. *King Bidgood's in the Bathtub.* Harcourt, 1985.

Wood, Audrey. *Silly Sally.* Harcourt, 1992.